ENDORSI

MW00532936

Never before have the attacks of the devil against the entire human race been so deadly. But Messiah's power in you is greater than any weapon of the devil. Most believers need an experienced teacher who has walked the walk, and this help has arrived! Becky Dvorak has written a timeless book filled with prophetic prayers and declarations that produce divine healing. Get this book, and activate His power to heal the sick, raise the dead, and release those creative miracles in you.

SID ROTH
Host of *It's Supernatural!*

Health is the greatest wealth. Becky is a true disciple of Jesus Christ. It is time for the Church to speak forth the oracles and prophetic Scriptures of God. Accept and perform the revelations contained in this book and walk in divine health in the Name of Jesus.

PASTOR DWIGHT DUNBAR
Work of God Church, Mitchell, IN

I love Becky's new book, *Decrees that Heal.* It's a powerhouse of resource and knowledge to teach us that the Word was made flesh and dwelt among His people to show us the Father's heart. He now dwells inside of the believer and the power of His spoken word will not return void, and always reflects the Father's heart for us. This puts this fact in a new light for us helping us to use and release the unlimited divine power Jesus died, bought, and paid for. This book is backed with Scripture, not anyone's opinion. You must know the truth to be set free, and even more important, speak the truth over your family and every situation that arises in your life. Becky helps us do just that with powerful confessions of truth backed by His word, which cannot fail.

APOSTLE DON GRAY
PASTOR SHARI GRAY
Passion Ecclesia Church, Kannapolis, NC

I have had the blessing and privilege of knowing and loving Becky Dvorak for a period of just one year, yet I share her heart as she brings hope and healing to the sick and afflicted in this world. I am blessed beyond measure by Becky's excellence as both a minister of the Gospel and an accomplished author. I so enjoyed reading her new book, *Decrees that Heal*, and found it to hold a personal touch that is inspiring and comforting to the reader. For those who are being challenged with sickness and disease, this book provides the ability to identify the destructive lies of the enemy. It is also a wonderful source of anointed prayers and confessions that will undergird your faith and bring healing and health to your body and mind as you declare them daily. As a pastor of almost forty years, I can say without reservation that Becky carries one of the greatest anointings that our church has ever experienced. Thank You, Lord Jesus, for this anointed woman of God!

JOAN BOETHEL
Co-Founder and Pastor of Bastrop Christian
Outreach Center, Bastrop, Texas
Joan Boethel Ministries, Inc.

Decrees *that* HEAL

DESTINY IMAGE BOOKS BY BECKY DVORAK

Dare to Believe

Greater than Magic

The Healing Creed

The Prophetic & Healing Power of Your WORDS

Conquering the Spirit of Death

The Waves of Healing Glory

Decrees *that* HEAL

*Prophetic Prayers & Declarations
that Bring Divine Healing*

BECKY DVORAK

© Copyright 2024–Becky Dvorak

All rights reserved. This book is protected by the copyright laws of the United States of America. This book may not be copied or reprinted for commercial gain or profit. The use of short quotations or occasional page copying for personal or group study is permitted and encouraged. Permission will be granted upon request. Scripture quotations marked NKJV are taken from the New King James Version. Copyright © 1982 by Thomas Nelson, Inc. Used by permission. All rights reserved. Scripture quotations marked AMP are taken from the Amplified® Bible, Copyright © 2015 by The Lockman Foundation, La Habra, CA 90631. All rights reserved. Used by permission. Scripture quotations marked KJV are taken from the King James Version. Scripture quotations marked NASB are taken from the NEW AMERICAN STANDARD BIBLE®, Copyright © 1960, 1962, 1963, 1968, 1971, 1972, 1973, 1975, 1977, 1995, 2020 by The Lockman Foundation. Used by permission. Scripture quotations marked NIV are taken from the HOLY BIBLE, NEW INTERNATIONAL VERSION®, Copyright © 1973, 1978, 1984, 2011 International Bible Society. Used by permission of Zondervan. All rights reserved. Scripture quotations marked NLT are taken from the Holy Bible, New Living Translation, copyright 1996, 2004, 2015. Used by permission of Tyndale House Publishers, Wheaton, Illinois 60189. All rights reserved. Scripture quotations marked ESV are taken from The Holy Bible, English Standard Version® (ESV®), copyright © 2001 by Crossway, a publishing ministry of Good News Publishers. Used by permission. All rights reserved. Take note that the name satan and related names are not capitalized. We choose not to acknowledge him, even to the point of violating grammatical rules.

DESTINY IMAGE® PUBLISHERS, INC.

P.O. Box 310, Shippensburg, PA 17257-0310

"Publishing cutting-edge prophetic resources to supernaturally empower the body of Christ"

This book and all other Destiny Image and Destiny Image Fiction books are available at Christian bookstores and distributors worldwide.

For more information on foreign distributors, call 717-532-3040.

Reach us on the Internet: www.destinyimage.com.

ISBN 13 TP: 978-0-7684-7580-7

ISBN 13 eBook: 978-0-7684-7581-4

For Worldwide Distribution, Printed in the U.S.A.

1 2 3 4 5 6 7 8 / 28 27 26 25 24

DEDICATION

This work is dedicated to all my students from around the world. It has been my honor to disciple you in the healing word and power of God. I take joy in all your accomplishments in the faith, and I can only imagine how pleased and proud God is of you.

ACKNOWLEDGMENTS

I want to give a big shout of thanks to Destiny Image Publishers for doing a great job to help me put this message, *Decrees that Heal*, before your eyes and into your heart. And a special thanks to Larry Sparks (publisher), Angela R. Shears (editor), Eileen Rockwell (cover designer), Terry Clifton (page designer), and Christian Raffetto (production manager). I am blessed to work with such a great team of professionals. I appreciate your gifts.

CONTENTS

Foreword 1

Preface. 3

A Word of Exhortation from Jehovah Rapha 5

SECTION 1   Teaching and Exhortation 9

PART 1   People Need Hope and Faith for Healing 10

PART 2   Expect That Miracle 25

PART 3   The Body of Christ Is Under Attack 35

PART 4   How Does the Prayer of Faith Work? 40

SECTION 2   Prayers and Confessions of Faith against
Sickness and Disease 45

PART 1   Autoimmune Disorders 47

PART 2   Blood Disorders 72

PART 3   Brain Disorders. 78

PART 4   Cancers. 91

PART 5   Death. 110

PART 6   Ear Conditions/Diseases 115

PART 7   Eye Conditions/Diseases .123

PART 8   Female Disorders 133

PART 9   Fungal Infections 152

PART 10   Genetic Conditions and Disorders 155

PART 11   Heart Disease 158

PART 12   Liver Diseases 169

PART 13   Lung Disease/Respiratory Illness. 174

PART 14   Male Disorders 186

PART 15   Mental Health Disorders 192

PART 16   Mosquito-Borne Diseases. .201

PART 17   Mouth Conditions/Diseases 206

PART 18   Nerve Damage 210

PART 19   Neurodegenerative Diseases. 214

PART 20   Neurological Disorders 221

PART 21   Nose/Sinuses 224

PART 22   Pancreas Disorders. 227

PART 23   Parasites 231

PART 24   Parathyroid Disease 234

PART 25   Sexually Transmitted Diseases 236

PART 26   Skin Conditions 244

PART 27   Sleep Disorders 249

PART 28   Speech Disorders 252

PART 29   Thyroid Diseases. 254

PART 30   Tick-Borne Diseases. 258

PART 31   Viral Infections. 262

PART 32   Waterborne Diseases 265

                Index 271

FOREWORD

Every once in a while we are faced with some simple truths from the Bible that completely change our perspective of how the Word is supposed to work. Becky Dvorak's book, *Decrees that Heal*, is one of those books.

Every Christian needs to understand that our enemy has only one tool that he uses to engage us in battle: deception! Once we hear the lie, we will eventually walk in that lie and receive it to be the truth to the detriment of our Christian walk. We want to receive healing and all the miracles that come from believing the Bible to be true and Jesus to be faithful to His Word. This book will open up your understanding of God's Word and confirm who you are in Christ and what belongs to you.

Healing, deliverance, and freedom are yours when you walk in your authority as a child of God.

Dr. Marilyn Hickey

PREFACE

The purpose of this work is not to tell you what to do or not to do medically, but to teach you how to pray in faith for those you know who are suffering from sickness and disease, and to give to you personal decrees and declarations of faith to confess over the health and wellbeing of your own body. It's my joy to give you these supernatural tools—*Decrees that Heal*.

A WORD OF EXHORTATION FROM JEHOVAH RAPHA

Have you been diagnosed with a disease that the medical field says there is no cure for? Are you ready to trash that hopeless medical report and not just go to another doctor for a second opinion, but go to the Doctor of all doctors and get the original report? Let's read a portion of this original report together.

First of all, I would like to introduce Myself to you: I am Jehovah Rapha, and I am the Lord who heals you (Exodus 15:26). I have redeemed you from this curse by becoming the curse for you (Galatians 3:13). How did I accomplish this? I was flogged at the whipping post where I shed My blood to purchase your healing (Isaiah 53:4-5). You wonder why I did this for you? Because I have loved you with an everlasting love (Jeremiah 31:3 NIV). I have promised to sustain, refresh, and to strengthen you on that bed of sickness (Psalm 41:3). I tell you not to be grieved and depressed, for My joy is your strength (Nehemiah 8:10 AMP). I say, "Take your spiritual medicine, and have yourself a good laugh" (Proverbs 17:22). Laugh a lot, and laugh no matter how you feel.

Bless Me, and don't forget all My benefits: I forgive all your iniquities, and I heal all your diseases (Psalm 103:2-3). No weapon formed against you shall prosper (Isaiah 54:17). No evil will conquer you; no plague will come near your home (Psalm 91:10 NLT). Serve Me, the Lord your God, and I will bless your bread and your water; and I will remove sickness from your midst (Exodus 23:25 NASB).

Have I not commanded you? Be strong and of good courage; do not be afraid, nor be dismayed, for I, the Lord your God am with you wherever you go (Joshua 1:9). For I have not given you a spirit of fear, but of power and of love and of a sound mind (2 Timothy 1:7). I, like you, have partaken of flesh and blood, and by My death I destroyed him who had the power of death, that is the devil, and I released you from that lifetime bondage of the fear of death (Hebrews 2:14-15). Remember, greater am I, Jesus, who is in you, than he (satan) who is in this world (1 John 4:4).

Whose report will you choose to believe (Isaiah 53:1)? They say, "Impossible!" but I declare, "With Me all things are possible!" (Mark 10:27). You decide—the decision is yours to make. I tell you in my Word, "Don't give place to the devil!" (Ephesians 4:27). I warn you that he is the father of all lies; there is no truth in him (John 8:44). The devil is a thief; he is out to steal, to kill, and to destroy your life (John 10:10), and with all cunning he lies and whispers to you to accept death. But I challenge you with this: *"Today I have given you the choice between life and death, between blessings and curses. Now I call on heaven and earth to witness the choice you make. Oh, that you would choose life, so that you and your descendants might live!"* (Deuteronomy 30:19 NLT).

You think to yourself, *Ah, but God, You are the great I am, You are all-powerful, You can't possibly understand what I am going through. After all, I am just a human.* I respond back to you with the Word of Truth (John 17:17). For you do not have a High Priest who cannot sympathize with your weaknesses, but was in all points tempted as you are, yet without sin (Hebrews 4:15). You see, I know you. I knew you before you were conceived inside your mother's womb. I know you better than you know yourself (Psalm 139:13-16). I created you in My image (Genesis 1:26-28), and I equipped you with all my authority over satan and all his wicked works (Luke 10:19). I gave you what I have, the power of life and death in your words (Proverbs 18:21).

I do not expect you to do this by your own strength, but believe Me when I say, "It is not by might nor by power, but by My Spirit," says the Lord of hosts (Zechariah 4:6). For the weapons of your warfare are not carnal but mighty in God for pulling down of strongholds (2 Corinthians 10:4). You overcome by the blood of the Lamb and by the words of your testimony (Revelation 12:11). These words have also been declared over you, "You are more than a conqueror" (Romans 8:37), and you shall do valiantly (Psalm 108:13). So fight the good fight of faith (1 Timothy 6:12), for everyone who has been born of Me overcomes the world. This is the victory that has overcome the world—your faith (1 John 5:4).

With love and mercy
from Jehovah Rapha,
the Lord who heals you

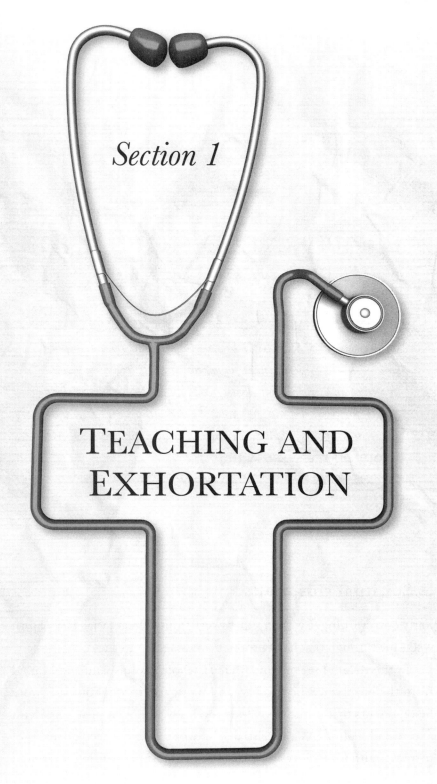

Section 1

TEACHING AND EXHORTATION

9

Part 1

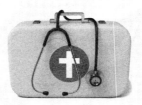

PEOPLE NEED HOPE AND FAITH FOR HEALING

WORD OF THE LORD: *"I believe in you and have equipped you with the supernatural power of faith to walk in divine healing and miracles. Trust Me when I say this healing is for you. I paid for your health and wellbeing with the power of My blood, because you are precious to Me."*
—YOUR HEALER, JESUS CHRIST

A Spiritual Hospital

Early one morning, I wake up in a sweat from a dream that Holy Spirit walks me through that has a prophetic message for us today.

In this dream I see my son, Marcos, whom my husband and I raised from the dead when he was just an infant, and throughout this work he represents that miracle you long for. I now see my ministry assistant and friend, Palma. As a Christian, she worked in the secular realm of mental health for twenty-five years. For the most part she felt frustrated with the medical field as she was not allowed to offer what the patients needed the most—hope from a Savior who could heal them. And then there is me, a woman of faith who does not have the medical training but the faith to believe for the miraculous. Let us journey through this dream together and hear what the Spirit of God, our supernatural compass, would say to us this day.

At first, I think we are entering into a hospital building, but I soon realize that this is not a hospital made by human hands, but a spiritual one. And as a healing evangelist, I am being shown the condition of the people and the cause for the condition.

As I set foot inside, I observe the people, who are many, waiting for someone to attend them, help them, and offer them a little hope that all will be well. But they seek this help for hope from the wrong source. Instead of turning to the Great Physician, Jesus, who is our only hope, they turn to the world's system that is utterly broken and in ruins.

We walk in together but are quickly separated and absorbed into the midst of the crowd. The needs of the people are so great. Immediately, I find myself standing in the reception room. The place is overrun with sick and dying people. I see a nurse who is feeling overwhelmed and standing near the reception desk. She calls aloud a three-letter code requesting assistance. Being surrounded by the people, I call out to the nurse and say, "I'm not a nurse, and I don't understand what that means." In a mocking tone, she laughs aloud and says, "That's obvious, had you been a nurse you would understand what it means." I respond, "I'm not here to cause trouble, but I am here to help."

Now we can take offense by the response of this nurse, or we can choose to look beyond the sarcastic comments and seek to understand. It's not uncommon for people who are overwhelmed and overworked, as these professionals have been, to be curt with others. And we should also consider that with all the death they have witnessed many could be suffering from PTSD (Post Traumatic Stress Disorder). We need to consider that there is often a great rift between the medical field and people of faith. Regardless, let us uphold our witness without compromise and reach out to those in need.

> *Let your light shine before men in such a way that they may see your good deeds and moral excellence, and [recognize and honor and] glorify your Father who is in heaven* (Matthew 5:16 AMP).

Proverbs 13:12 (NIV) says this about hope, or the lack of hope: *"Hope deferred makes the heart sick, but a longing fulfilled is a tree of life."*

Hope is a supernatural power given to us by God. It's the expectation to believe for something better. It is also the forerunner to faith. Hebrews 11:1 (NKJV) says it to us in this manner: *"Now faith is the substance of things hoped for, the evidence of things not seen."* Without hope, or expectation, we are unable to move into the realm of faith, and another way to consider faith is to trust. In this dream, the people were not able to trust or have faith in God, because hope, or their expectation for wellness, was deferred. Today it is often denied, and this makes the heart sick. It causes the situation or the sickness to grow worse, and it can even be deadly.

Therefore, we need to hold on to hope, which is life-giving; it's where miracles begin. Guard it as if our life depends upon it, as it often does.

> *Let us hold unswervingly to the hope we profess, for he who promised is faithful* (Hebrews 10:23 NIV).

Let's take a moment and consider this word *unswervingly*. With my mind's eye, I see a visual of a drunk driver swerving from lane to lane as they try to hug that center line, but because they are drunk they can't stay in their lane. And this state of being is dangerous and often deadly. This is how it is in the spirit realm. When we are filled with worldly views concerning faith and God's healing power, it's difficult and next to impossible to stay on that straight and narrow path where we trust and believe God. This too is a dangerous and deadly way to live.

Prayer

Dear Holy Spirit,

In the mighty name of Jesus, the author and finisher of my faith, I ask for Your help, starting now, to hold on to the hope found only in You that I profess to have. May I not swerve to the right or to the left but stay on that straight and narrow pathway that leads to You and Your faithfulness to keep that healing promise to me. In the precious name of the Lord, Jesus Christ, I pray, amen.

A Spiritual Inspection

I should add, besides the look of hopelessness upon the faces of the people in my dream, the walls and the condition of this hospital have their own story to tell as well.

Like a spiritual building inspector, I can't help but notice that the walls are incomplete and very dirty, the flooring is busted up, the furnishings are destroyed, the place is in shambles, and the further I go inside the worse it gets. As I continue this spiritual tour, it is very evident that the people have lost the light, as the atmosphere becomes darker and darker.

What can we gain from the inspection of this spiritual building? That the foundations of faith for many are in a hazardous state of being. Yes, they are faulty, weak, and falling apart. We need to start over, and this time lay a firm foundation, rebuild the walls, and build it to last.

People of Faith Have a Great Capacity to Believe

People of faith have a great capacity to believe for amazing things not yet seen, and some can believe more readily for the miraculous than others. Your faith might not be at the level *yet* where you can believe anything is possible, but their faith is, and yours can be. Perhaps it's because you have not been beaten down by the devil with such evil attacks against your body, but because they have, they have flung themselves into the loving arms of Jesus and made the bold decision to believe no matter what. They don't want to die but live. And they know the only hope for true healing flows from the redemptive blood of our Lord and Savior, Jesus Christ. It's beyond me why we would discourage any person from believing God to bring that thing in the earthly realm of impossible into the spiritual realm of reality. After all, Jesus does proclaim in Mark 10:27 (NKJV), *"With men it is impossible, but not with God; for with God all things are possible."*

Are You Being Buffeted by Demons?

You might be thinking to yourself, *I agree that with God all things are possible, but I'm not there. And the way things are going, I don't know if I ever will arrive to that level of faith. It's been one attack after another, and I can't seem to rise above it all.* If this is you, it could be that your body is being buffeted by demons as the apostle Paul was, but you have not activated your faith for supernatural healing that flows from the throne of grace. You may be confused by false doctrine from the religious sector that accuses God of putting sickness on Paul, such as blindness, and that he endured with joy over this God-given thorn in the flesh against his body. Let's bring correction to this false teaching so that you can be free from the ill effects of it.

> *And lest I should be exalted above measure through the abundance of the revelations, there was given to me a thorn in the flesh, the messenger of Satan to buffet me, lest I should be exalted above measure. For this thing I besought the Lord thrice, that it might depart from me. And he said unto me, My grace is sufficient for thee: for my strength*

is made perfect in weakness. Most gladly therefore will I rather glory in my infirmities, that the power of Christ may rest upon me. Therefore I take pleasure in infirmities, in reproaches, in necessities, in persecutions, in distresses for Christ's sake: for when I am weak, then am I strong (2 Corinthians 12:7-10 KJV).

This portion of Scripture is talking about protecting Paul from becoming prideful and is not about God plaguing him with sickness or withholding healing from him as he begs God to take the thorn away from him. The *"thorn in the flesh"* is not sickness and disease such as blindness or any other type of eye disease, but a demon who buffets him—attacks Paul with one attack after another.

Many of God's people believe that He has given them a thorn in the flesh—by which they mean an illness intended to teach them a spiritual lesson in patience and endurance and to draw them closer to God. This is a lie from the devil himself. And this type of belief turns many away from God. They blame Him for the devil's work. It misconstrues their conception of Almighty God as one who does not care but is cruel and harsh and on the lookout for an opportunity to punish His people. In fact, with the payment of His blood Jesus purchased our healing for us at the whipping post.

But [in fact] He has borne our griefs, and He has carried our sorrows and pains; yet we [ignorantly] assumed that He was stricken, struck down by God and degraded and humiliated [by Him]. But He was wounded for our transgressions, He was crushed for our wickedness [our sin, our injustice, our wrongdoing]; the punishment [required] for our well-being fell on Him, and by His stripes (wounds) we are healed (Isaiah 53:4-5 AMP).

Biblical Facts from Isaiah 53:4-5

Jesus bore our griefs. This word *griefs* means sickness (Strong's H2483). And what did He do with our sicknesses at Calvary? He bore them. This means our Lord carried them for us (Strong's H5375).

This foundational portion of Scripture continues to explain what the Lord did for us. It says that He carried our sorrows, or He bore them for us on His back. And just what are those sorrows? Physical and mental pain (Strong's H4341).

It goes on to say that we esteem or judge Him (Strong's H2803) stricken, plagued (Strong's H5060), smitten, slaughtered (Strong's H5221) by God. Because Jesus was wounded, defiled (Strong's H2490) for our transgressions—our rebellion (Strong's H6588). He was bruised, crushed (Strong's H1792) for our iniquities, our perversity, our sin (Strong's H5771).

The chastisement, discipline, or correction (Strong's H4148) for our peace, our welfare, health, and prosperity (Strong's H7965) was upon Him. And by His stripes, bruises, and wounds (Strong's H2250) we are healed, cured, and made whole (Strong's H7495).

(These definitions are taken from the chart on pages 37-38 in Chapter 3, "The Power of the Blood," from my book *The Healing Creed*. We will refer to this chart and the meaning of these powerful verses throughout this work.)

He Understands the Frailty of Humanness

Our Lord understands the frailty of our humanness. Remember, He chose to leave His God-powers in heaven and walk this earth in human form and, like us, face the same temptations and hardships and make the same type of daily decisions we face today: "Do I believe that with God this seemingly impossible situation can turn around? Do I deny this great healing power and cling to my human reasoning of unbelief?"

I believe as you continue to call out to the Lord with an honest plea about what's going on inside your soul, that barrier between you and God will start to come down, and that urgent cry for help to believe again will be answered. With time spent in prayer and in the Word, your faith will be strengthened once again.

Taste the Goodness of the Lord

You may have had a taste of religion, which has a foul flavor mixed with a bit of spiritual sugar, such as, "God is good, He loves you, but He's testing your faithfulness with that cancerous tumor." You see what I mean? It leaves a bitter aftertaste in the mouth. It's time to spit that out and get a real taste of the goodness of God, who has good things in store for you and truly desires to fellowship with you.

David prays this encouraging verse found in Psalm 34:8 (AMP), *"O taste and see that the Lord [our God] is good; how blessed [fortunate, prosperous, and favored by God] is the man who takes refuge in Him."* We are to perceive—become aware of by personal experience—the goodness of God so that we can come to believe that His nature is good, and He only has our best interests in mind.

The prophet Nahum, in the book named after him found in the Old Testament, writes this about God's character during a time of great tribulation for his nation, while they were being ruled by an evil king: *"The Lord is good, a stronghold in the day of trouble, and He knows those who take refuge in Him"* (Nahum 1:7 NASB). This word *stronghold* in *Strong's Concordance* means a place of safety, protection and refuge (Strong's H4581). The goodness of God provides these things for us, and in His presence is where we find His protection.

Psalm 84 is a beautiful psalm about the goodness and faithfulness of God. In verse 11 it says, *"For the Lord God is our sun and our shield. He gives us grace and glory. The Lord will withhold no good thing from those who do what is right"* (Psalm 84:11 NLT). The author of this psalm speaks of the good things, the blessings of God that He gifts to those who enter the presence of God. He knows them, and He showers them with the necessities of life. Perhaps as you read this, you yourself are in great need for healing. Enter His presence with a heart of worship, be thankful for who He is, and allow Him to supply the need that you have.

Five Dangerous Lies People Are Taught to Believe

As you can tell, I am not a fan of religion, and quite frankly neither was Jesus. I have heard people share the most devastating lies that they were told by people who claim to be Christians and say they know the Word of God but spread the most outlandish lies to hurt people. I'm going to share a list of common lies that I hear from people needing a healing touch from the Lord.

Because you are sick, you must have done something wicked.

Just because someone is very sick does not mean they have done something wicked. Yes, sin does open the door to the enemy's attack, but oftentimes these attacks of sickness come because we live in a fallen world. Jesus lets us know in John 16:33 (NKJV), *"These things I have spoken to you, that in Me you may have peace. In the world you will have tribulation; but be of good cheer, I have overcome the world."* When He says that you will have tribulation, He means you will have difficult times. Not because God has designed your journey on this earth to be filled with bad things, but because you have an enemy, satan, who is bent upon your destruction. Jesus says this about the devil in John 10:10 (NKJV), *"The thief does not come except to steal, and to kill, and to destroy. I have come that they may have life, and that they may have it more abundantly."*

Supernatural healing is not for today.

This is an especially dangerous lie to spread. I wonder just how many people have died needlessly because of it. God says of Himself, *"I am the Lord who heals you"* (Exodus 15:26 NKJV). Matthew 8:17 states this biblical fact, *"He Himself took our infirmities and bore our sicknesses."* We can rest assured that He has not removed supernatural healing from His list of goodness toward us, as it says in Hebrews 13:8 (NKJV), *"Jesus Christ is the same yesterday, today, and forever."* And again, in Malachi 3:6 (NKJV) we read, *"For I am the Lord, I do not change."* Simply put, healing is for today. God has not removed His healing promises from the New Covenant.

My needs are trivial and unimportant to God.

You are important to God, and He cares about every detail in your life. Here's a verse about how deeply He cares about the little details concerning you: *"But the very hairs of your head are all numbered. Do not fear therefore, you are of more value than many sparrows"* (Luke 12:7 NKJV). *"Look at the birds of the air, for they neither sow nor reap nor gather into barns; yet your heavenly Father feeds them. Are you not of more value than they?"* (Matthew 6:26 NKJV). And here is another portion of Scripture to help you know God considers you very valuable to Him: *"How precious also are Your thoughts to me, O God! How great is the sum of them! If I should count them, they would be more in number than the sand; when I awake, I am still with You"* (Psalm 139:17-18 NKJV).

It's God's will that you are sick.

This is not what my Bible says! John writes in 3 John 1:2 (NKJV), *"Beloved, I pray that you may prosper in all things and be in health, just as your soul prospers."* So the next time someone says this to you, you rebuke them and say, "No, it's not! With the shed blood of Jesus at the whipping post, and throughout the entire atoning process, I have been redeemed, my sins are forgiven, and my body has been healed too" (see Isaiah 53:4-5).

Prayer doesn't change much.

Let me be clear—not all communication with God is prayer. A lot of what is said is whining and complaining, and you're right—that doesn't move God. Only faith moves God. So when we pray, we are to pray in faith, without whining, complaining, blaming Him for evil, and without doubt and unbelief. This is what faith-filled prayers accomplish, *"And the prayer of faith will save the sick, and the Lord will raise him up. And if he has committed sins, he will be forgiven"* (James 5:15 NKJV). Now, this verse alone undoes all the lies mentioned under this subtitle.

Have you been taught a dangerous lie that is preventing you from receiving your supernatural healing? Take some time to pray about this question, write it down, and look up one to three verses from the Bible to undo the lie that was planted within your mind and emotions.

_____

_____

_____

_____

_____

_____

If God says it, that settles it! He declares that by His stripes you are healed and that this healing power is for anyone who chooses to believe in it. Don't allow anyone to talk you out of your right to be healed in Jesus' name.

Personal Reflection

Go through the five lies that people are taught to believe. Have you been taught to believe any of these lies? If so, do they hinder your ability to trust and believe God for your healing? What are you going to do about the lie that is blocking your healing from manifesting?

Group Discussion

Together as a group, discuss the five lies that people are taught to believe and how they hinder our ability to trust God to heal our bodies.

We have tackled quite a bit in this first chapter, and now it's time to turn to the next chapter and ask ourselves, "Are we really expecting this miracle from God? Or are we just hoping that it will happen?"

Questions for Part 1

1. According to Proverbs 13:12, what makes the heart sick?

2. Hebrews 11:1 says what about the substance of faith?

3. What do we need to do with hope?

4. What does Mark 10:27 tell us is possible with God?

5. According to 2 Corinthians 12:7-10, what was Paul's thorn in the flesh?

6. In this portion of Scripture, Paul is being protected from what?

7. Is Paul's thorn in the flesh an eye disease or any other type of illness?

8. According to Isaiah 53:5 we are what?

9. What is the meaning of the word *healed*?

10. Our Lord understands the frailty of what?

11. In Psalm 84:11, we read that for those who do what's right, our God will not withhold what?

Answers for Part 1

1. *Hope deferred.*

2. *That it is the evidence of things not seen.*

3. *Guard it as if our life depends upon it, as it often does.*

4. *All things.*

5. *A demon sent to buffet him.*

6. *Becoming prideful.*

7. *No.*

8. *Healed.*

9. *Cured and made whole.*

10. *Our humanness.*

11. *Any good thing.*

Faith is trust. You can have such bold faith when you trust God. And faith is the only way to please Him. He wills that we come boldly before His throne of grace. We can whine and complain and even blame God for the problems in our life. Adam and Eve did this in the Garden of Eden (see Genesis 3:12-19). Adam blamed Eve, then Eve blamed the devil. But did their situation change for the better after they blamed the devil for their disobedience? No, it did not.

How about the Israelites when they wandered in the wilderness? They murmured and complained about everything. Did that move God to get them out of that situation? No, it did not. They wandered in that wilderness for forty years. (You can read about this true story in the Book of Exodus.) They just didn't quite get the fact that God isn't moved by our negative emotional outbursts or our accusing words against Him. So what does move Him and get His face to turn our way if these temper tantrums do not work? Faith does. He gravitates to people of faith.

> *But without faith it is impossible to please Him, for he who comes to God must believe that He is, and that He is a rewarder of those who diligently seek Him* (Hebrews 11:6 NKJV).

So allow me to ask you again, "Are you expecting that miracle?" I believe for many of you that miracle is on the verge of manifesting. But you must get out of the waiting room and into that birthing room. You need to step out of the realm of just hoping for that miracle to manifest to where you are expecting it to manifest.

You can wait and wait for the manifestation of that miracle to happen, but it won't—not until you move out of the realm of hope and into the realm of faith where you expect that miracle to take place.

I am a mother of eight, and I gave birth to three; the others were adopted. Each pregnancy and birth was different, but here is one thing that was the same each time. Shortly before giving birth, something would happen to me, as it does with all mothers—a nesting instinct would rise within me. I had to make sure everything I could do, I did. Every nook and cranny in our home had to be scrubbed with everything neatly in its place. Basically, nothing was left undone, and I remained in preparation mode until I accomplished it all. Then, shortly after that time of making ready for that miracle, that child to come—they did.

It's the same way in the supernatural realm of faith. You first are hopeful, then you move into the next phase of expectancy, you prepare for delivery day, and finally the miracle manifests.

Let's Pray

Father God,

Right now, in the name of Jesus, I renounce this sickness and this disease attacking these people. I pray in faith, believing without wavering with doubt and unbelief that You have already released the power of Your blood to heal each one reading this prayer of faith. By Your stripes, those healing whips You bore upon Your back to purchase healing for all, were not in vain, but their healings manifest fully, leaving nothing undone. All this I pray for the glory of the Lord, amen.

Lies That Women Are Taught to Believe

To help you step into the arena of faith for your miracle, I want to look at lies that women are taught to believe that have the power to stop that healing from manifesting before it has a chance to even begin.

God cannot forgive an unwed mother; therefore, she cannot receive the benefits of God, including healing.

Now, where does the Bible say this? Nowhere! But what does God's Word say about forgiveness? *"If we confess our sins, He is faithful and just to forgive us our sins and to cleanse us from all unrighteousness"* (1 John 1:9 NKJV).

A divorced woman is to be shunned, forever guilty, and deserves to be sick. She's unclean and not worthy to receive God's blessings, such as healing.

I remember one such woman who was in an AIDS hospice. Her family and members of the church she belonged to would not come to visit her or show her any type of support because she was very sick with HIV. They never took into consideration that it was her husband who was unfaithful, infected her with this disease, and then left her for a younger woman. She was treated unfairly and made to feel like an outcast among family and friends. But was she an outcast to God? She was told that she was, and she believed what they said to her. But what does God's Word have to say to this woman, or to any woman who finds themselves in a similar situation?

> *For your husband is your Maker, the Lord of hosts is His name; and your Redeemer is the Holy One of Israel, who is called the God of the whole earth* (Isaiah 54:5 AMP).
>
> *So do not fear, for I am with you; do not be dismayed, for I am your God. I will strengthen you and help you; I will uphold you with my righteous right hand* (Isaiah 41:10 NIV).
>
> *Come to me, all you who are weary and burdened, and I will give you rest. Take my yoke upon you and learn from me, for I am gentle and humble in heart, and you will find rest for your souls. For my yoke is easy and my burden is light* (Matthew 11:28-30 NIV).
>
> *"For I will restore health to you and I will heal your wounds,"* *says the Lord* (Jeremiah 30:17 AMP).

Ask Holy Spirit to show you if there is a lie that is preventing you from trusting the Lord for your divine healing from Jesus. If He reveals a lie to you, write it down, and look up one to three verses from the

Bible to undo the power of that lie that was planted within your mind and emotions.

_____

_____

_____

_____

_____

_____

Throughout the Gospels, we read how Jesus broke all religious barriers to heal the people. So why would we then put up barriers that prevent people to come and be healed?

Remember, God's Word is truth, and health and healing are good gifts from God for your benefit. Don't allow anyone to steal them from you by telling you lies.

Personal Reflection

This chapter is loaded with undeniable faith, and I must examine my own heart and ask myself the hard question, "Am I expecting that miracle?" I want to be, but am I? And if I'm not quite there yet, am I willing to do what is necessary to get there?

Group Discussion

With your group, discuss the main question, "Am I expecting that miracle?" Allow each member to share from their heart where they think they are. Some will say, "Yes!" Others will struggle to admit that they aren't where they should be but want to be. Pray for one another; encourage them in the faith that they can get to this point in their walk with the Lord if they want to.

We've been through an amazing chapter of faith in which we asked ourselves the hard question, "Am I expecting that miracle?" Now we're going to take it a step further and learn to call that miracle into existence.

Questions for Part 2

1. What is God waiting for?

2. What happens when we obey God and do things His way?

3. What is faith?

4. What is the only way to please God?

5. Did Adam and Eve's situation change after they blamed God?

6. What was it that the Israelites didn't quite get about God as they wandered in the wilderness for 40 years?

7. God gravitates to what type of people?

8. You can wait and wait for the manifestation of that miracle to happen, but it won't until you do what?

Answers for Part 2

1. *For you to line up to the Word of God and for you to do it His way.*

2. *The blessings of God come upon us, and they just don't come upon us, they chase us down.*

3. *Trust.*

4. *By faith.*

5. *No.*

6. *God isn't moved by our negative emotional outbursts or our accusing words against Him.*

7. *People of faith.*

8. *Move out of the realm of hope and into the realm of faith where you expect that miracle to take place.*

Part 3

THE BODY OF CHRIST IS UNDER ATTACK

The further I walk through this dream with Holy Spirit, the stranger and more startling things become. As I follow Him into the next room, I sense great danger, and I begin to call out for my son, Marcos. I know it is not safe for him, a young Christian man of faith, to be in this place. I look up and I see another young man trying to strangle him. I call out, "Marcos!" and he responds and says, "I'm alright, he's just praying for me." I answered and said, "No, he's not. He's trying to kill you!" What is this other man trying to do to my son? He is trying to strangle the life of God out of him. He is trying to kill his faith.

I understand that Marcos represents several things in this dream. For one, he is our son we raised from the dead, so he symbolizes the manifestation of the supernatural power of God. I often experience firsthand the attack of false doctrine by the religious community to snuff out the miraculous power of God, and this is what I am witnessing. He also represents how the enemy is trying to destroy the masculinity of our young men. The mentally deranged are trying to overpower the souls of men. My task in this portion of the dream is to be a watchman and put a stop to this attack.

Holy Spirit, What Is Going On?

Midway through the dream, I hear myself call out to Holy Spirit, "Am I sick? Do I have a high fever and delirium from it? Is this why I am having a nightmare?" I hear Holy Spirit's voice call back to me, "No, it's because you are under attack."

You may be questioning Holy Spirit, "What is going on?" If you are, you are not alone—many people are. There is an answer. We are under attack. Jesus makes it clear to us in John 10:10 (NKJV) when He says, *"The thief does not come except to steal, and to kill, and to destroy."* The enemy knows his time is short and the demonic attacks are ramping up at a high-pitched fever against us. But nonetheless, greater is Jesus in us than satan in this world (see 1 John 14:4).

A Spiritual Darkness Like We Have Never Seen Before

Marcos and I now set foot into a dark, dank, and oppressive room, and a perverse man walks up to us and begins to speak unashamedly about his ungodly desires toward us. I say to Marcos, "We need to get out of here now!"

The Bible tells us that in these latter days it will be worse than it was in the days of Noah. This world is full of sexual filth; it's all around us, and these vile spirits have come out of their closets and are on the warpath to openly pervert as many as they can and lead them to hell, especially the children and young people of our day.

> *When the Son of Man returns, it will be like it was in Noah's day. In those days before the flood, the people were enjoying banquets and parties and weddings right up to the time Noah entered his boat. People didn't realize what was going to happen until the flood came and swept them all away. That*

is the way it will be when the Son of Man comes (Matthew 24:37-39 NLT).

For this reason God gave them up to dishonorable passions. For their women exchanged natural relations for those that are contrary to nature; and the men likewise gave up natural relations with women and were consumed with passion for one another, men committing shameless acts with men and receiving in themselves the due penalty for their error. And since they did not see fit to acknowledge God, God gave them up to a debased mind to do what ought not to be done (Romans 1:26-28 ESV).

The Vulnerable, Confused, and Hurt

After escaping this filthy, sin-filled room, we pass into an area full of vulnerable people. We no sooner arrive when a young man with Down Syndrome walks up to me and holds on tightly to my arm. I can tell by his behavior that he is afraid, as he's accustomed to being abused. He readily receives the godly protection that I offer, but suddenly his trust transforms into fear. While he looks up at me, he fearfully says, "I know you are going to hurt me." I reply, "No, I'm not." He says, "I know you are going to hurt me." I say to him again, "No, I'm not. And I would never hurt you." He continues muttering in fear that I am going to do him harm. Then suddenly a demon, "a lying spirit" that has been tormenting this young man, appears and is trying to spit in my face but is unable to produce the saliva to spit.

What is the Spirit of God revealing to me in this room? These lying spirits (demons) are misleading the vulnerable, weak, and feeble people with falsehoods that we the Church, the people of God, are not to be trusted and are going to do them harm. A veil of fear is over them, and they have been taught to be leery of the very ones who want to reach out and help them.

I realize we are all under attack, and this is more than just a dream—it is a prophetic message from the Lord to warn us of the season we live in. It's time for us to wake up and put our faith into action before it is too late.

Consider this: many years ago, Christ was falsely accused, mocked and spit upon, abused, abandoned, crucified, and buried in a tomb. The situation appeared to be without hope. The Servant's service was devalued, they twisted His message, the intentions of His heart were unjustly judged, they destroyed His reputation, and He was made out to be the evil one. What did Jesus do? He stretched out His arms and cried out, "Father, forgive them, for they know not what they do," and He gave them everything He had—Himself.

The spiritual body of Christ is under attack today. What do we do? Do we retreat in a corner and tremble with fear of what they might do to us? Or do we do what Jesus does—pray for the lost who are attacking and betraying Him? Be the light that shines in their darkness and give them everything we've got, Jesus. Use the supernatural power of faith and override their evil with God's good. Encourage the oppressed, deliver the possessed, heal the sick, and save the lost.

The world does not realize it, but they need us to be strong in the faith, spiritually equipped, and ready to be about our heavenly Father's business and to do His bidding the way Jesus demonstrates for us—through healing and miracles, signs, and wonders.

Together we, the Church, will accomplish this mission.

Personal Reflection

The body of Christ is under attack. What am I doing about it? Am I retreating in a corner? Am I trembling with fear of what they might do to me? Am I praying for the lost? Am I shining my light into their darkness? What am I doing?

one for whom He should do this was deserving, "for he loves our nation, and has built us a synagogue."

Then Jesus went with them. And when He was already not far from the house, the centurion sent friends to Him, saying to Him, "Lord, do not trouble Yourself, for I am not worthy that You should enter under my roof. Therefore I did not even think myself worthy to come to You. But say the word, and my servant will be healed. For I also am a man placed under authority, having soldiers under me. And I say to one, 'Go,' and he goes; and to another, 'Come,' and he comes; and to my servant, 'Do this,' and he does it."

When Jesus heard these things, He marveled at him, and turned around and said to the crowd that followed Him, "I say to you, I have not found such great faith, not even in Israel!" And those who were sent, returning to the house, found the servant well who had been sick.

We read that a certain centurion's servant, who was dear to him, is sick and ready to die. This centurion is a person of authority, and he understands how the power of authority operates. Through a messenger, he sends a message to Jesus, the Healer. Jesus receives the message and responds and is on His way to the centurion's home. I find verse 7 chock-full of great insight for us. As Jesus draws near, the centurion says, *"Therefore, I did not even think myself worthy to come to You. But say the word, and my servant will be healed."*

Four Important Points to the Centurion's Encounter with Jesus

1. The centurion recognizes that Jesus has great authority, even greater authority than he has.

41

2. As Jesus draws near, he feels unworthy and stops Jesus from drawing closer.

3. The physical distance between Jesus and his sick servant does not matter.

4. He knows the power of the spoken word.

Perhaps you find yourself in a similar situation to this centurion. Someone who is very special to you is very sick and dying. Whether you realize it or not, you are like this centurion. You are a person of great power, and the power you possess is authority. What are the words of Jesus in Luke 10:19 (AMP)? *"Listen carefully: I have given you authority [that you now possess] to tread on serpents and scorpions, and [the ability to exercise authority] over all the power of the enemy (Satan); and nothing will [in any way] harm you."*

Let's face it, that illness has a poisonous bite like a serpent, and it stings like a scorpion. But you have been given the authority of Christ over it. This is an amazing gift of power. Unfortunately for many, this power of authority lies dormant within you. It's time to wake up to the spiritual facts of life—that disease is lesser in power than Jesus in you (see 1 John 4:4). It's also time to activate this power of authority within you against the wicked wiles of the enemy, such as deadly attacks of premature death.

We should also address the fact that as Jesus draws near to him, he senses His holiness and feels unworthy. Throughout Scripture, this is a normal response when the Lord draws near to someone. But I want to note another spiritual fact or two here. Jesus is our righteousness, and when we approach the Father with a need, we are to come with boldness and with all confidence.

Hebrews 4:16 (NLT) says, *"So let us come boldly to the throne of our gracious God. There we will receive his mercy, and we will find grace to help us when we need it most."*

First John 5:14-15 (NASB) says it like this, *"This is the confidence which we have before Him, that, if we ask anything according to His will, He hears us. And if we know that He hears us in whatever we ask, we know that we have the requests which we have asked from Him."*

I appreciate the fact that this man of authority understands that this physical distance between Jesus and the centurion's servant doesn't matter. And I tell you the truth—a word spoken in faith is not bound by physical distance. In the spirit, there is no distance.

The centurion understands the power of words backed with authority, and we should too. When we pray these prayers of faith, we are not to just release a bunch of mumbo jumbo from our lips, but we are to boldly and confidently speak words of faith that release healing power into those we are praying for and believe without doubting that these individuals are healed in Jesus' name.

Personal Reflection

Do I understand the four important points about the centurion's encounter with Jesus? Do I recognize the greatness of His authority? Do I shy away from drawing near to Jesus because I feel unworthy? When it comes to matters of faith, do I understand that there is no distance in the spirit realm? Do I understand and operate in the power of the spoken word?

Group Discussion

With your group, discuss the four important points about the centurion's encounter with Jesus. Talk about the greatness of His authority. Openly discuss why we sometimes shy away from drawing near to Jesus. Talk about the fact that there is no distance in the spirit realm, and what this means in the realm of the miraculous. Do you understand and operate in the power of the spoken word?

Questions for Part 4

1. List four important points about the centurion's encounter with Jesus.

2. What does Jesus say to us in Luke 10:19?

Answers for Part 4

1. *He recognizes that Jesus has great authority, even greater authority than he has. As Jesus draws near, he feels unworthy, and stops Jesus from drawing closer. The physical distance between Jesus and his sick servant does not matter. He knows the power of the spoken word.*

2. *"Listen carefully: I have given you authority [that you now possess] to tread on serpents and scorpions, and [the ability to exercise authority] over all the power of the enemy (Satan); and nothing will [in any way] harm you"* (Luke 10:19 AMP).

these glands and into their ability to make an ample supply of these hormones. I believe it is the will of God to heal me of all disease and that my Father has no lack of hormones to supply my adrenal glands with. I praise the Lord that I serve the living God, and it is His will to heal me of all things, including this. I declare by faith that my body rehydrates supernaturally, that energy returns, nausea and vomiting stop, muscle and joint pains cease, that I gain the proper amount of weight for my body size and type, and that I will not die prematurely but live. I give glory and praise to Him for my life and healing, amen and amen.

Alopecia/Hair Loss

Prayer of Faith

I pray for you in faith, believing for creative, miracle-working power to flow through your immune system and command it to stop attacking your head of hair. I release this same healing virtue into your hair follicles, and where your hair is missing it grows back strong and healthy, with no more balding, amen.

Confession of Faith

I decree, in the name of the Lord, a separation between me and this autoimmune disease, alopecia. I am loosed from this infirmity (Luke 12:13) because You, Jesus, redeemed me from this curse by becoming the curse for me (Gal. 3:13). I declare, "No more hair loss, in Jesus' name!" I release the healing and life-giving power of the Lord to flow throughout my hair follicles to give them life and strength and declare that I have a full head of hair, amen.

Autoimmune Vasculitis

Prayer of Faith

In the name of Jesus, I renounce this spirit of death and the confusion of your immune system from damaging your blood vessels by the means of inflammation and wreaking havoc throughout your body. I release the power of the blood of Christ to flow through your blood vessels with healing to strengthen them and to restore them to their proper thickness so that the width of their passageways cannot restrict the flow of blood and damage your organs and tissues. I declare that this weapon formed against you will not prosper, and if organs and tissues have already been damaged, they are re-created, healed, made whole, and fully functional for the glory of the Lord, amen.

Confession of Faith

I believe in the power of the blood of Jesus to deliver me from this spirit of death attacking my blood vessels. I will not align my faith with this negative report. I activate my faith in the report of the Lord from Isaiah 53:4-5 that declares by His stripes I am already healed from this. And yes, I do believe in the healing power of the Lord and receive His healing power into my immune system to correct the way it functions. It will no longer attack my blood vessels with inflammation but help my blood vessels. I declare that my blood vessels are the correct thickness and that the width of their passageways cannot restrict the blood flow or cause damage to organs and tissues throughout my body. They will support them for long life. In His most precious name, I pray, amen.

Celiac Disease

Prayer of Faith

I come boldly before God's throne of grace presenting your need to Him (Heb. 14:6) and I declare by faith without wavering (Heb. 10:23) that by His healing stripes (Isa. 53:4-5) you are delivered from this spirit of death and Celiac disease and all the harm it is causing your body and to your life. I release the healing power of the blood of Jesus to flow through your immune system to re-create it so that it no longer reacts to the gluten in your food. I speak words of faith over your small intestine that it is cleansed from all impurities. The lining of this intestine and the villi that line the intestine are restored and fully functional. By faith, I declare that your villi can absorb vitamins, minerals, and other nutrients from the food you eat. All the negative side effects be gone, done away with in Jesus' name, amen.

Confession of Faith

Lord, I am strong and courageous, without fear or discouragement (Josh. 1:9). You are for me and not against me (Rom. 8:31). I trust You and Your Word, no matter what the negative report says or how my body reacts. Your Word declares that by Your healing whips I am healed (Isa. 53:4-5) and that my faith is the only evidence I need to know that I am healed (Heb. 11:1). With a decree of faith, I build a wall of protection between me and this spirit of death, Celiac disease. I accept Your healing power in my immune system, and command it to stop reacting to the gluten found in food. I declare all that You gave me—a healed small intestine, lining of the intestine, and the villi. My villi can absorb vitamins, minerals, and other nutrients from the food I eat. I am delivered from all negative side effects in Your most holy name, amen.

Chronic Allergies

Prayer of Faith

I pray in faith for you against chronic allergies. I decree that the control these allergies have over you is broken in your life (Gal. 3:13). I declare words of faith that you are loosed from this infirmity (Luke 12:13). By faith, your immune system is re-created and healed and no longer hypersensitive to harmless substances in Jesus' name, amen.

Confession of Faith

By my faith in the mightiest of all names, Jesus Christ (Ps. 148:13), I use the God-given power of my words (Prov. 18:21) and speak healing to my immune system against chronic allergies. My immune system recognizes the difference between a harmful invader and a harmless substance, and no longer does it overreact to harmless ones. By His stripes my skin, sinuses, airways and/or digestive system are no longer inflamed. I decree and it is established in my body (Job 22:27)—allergies do not control my life, and my immune system is not confused but aids in healing my body as God created it to do. I believe and receive His benefit of healing (Ps. 103:2-3). Amen.

Graves' Disease, Grave's Ophthalmopathy, Grave's Dermopathy

Prayer of Faith

On your behalf, I take a stand of faith against the overproduction of thyroid hormones coming against you. I release the healing power of the Lord Jesus to flow into your thyroid hormones and reduce the amount that your body produces to a normal and healthy quantity.

I renounce Grave's ophthalmopathy, the buildup of carbo-hydrates and the inflammation in the muscles and other tissues around your eyes. I speak healing into your eyes and that the bulging, gritty sensation; the pressure and pain; the redness, sensitivity to light, double vision, and even vision loss be healed and your eyes be made whole, free from Grave's ophthalmopathy.

In the name of Jesus, I rebuke Graves' dermopathy, the red-dening and thickening of the skin on your shins and the tops of your feet. I command them to be healed and made whole, amen.

Confession of Faith

I believe in the healing power of the Lord Jesus to heal me from an overproduction of thyroid hormones. I do not accept the labels of Grave's disease, Grave's ophthalmopathy, or Grave's dermopathy or their destructive power against me. I know that Jesus in me is greater than satan who is behind this disease (1 John 4:4). He is both able and willing to heal me (Luke 5:12-16). I believe in the power of creation (Gen. 1) and that my words possess the power of life and death (Prov. 18:21), and I use them wisely to speak life, healing, and re-cre-ation into my immune system, thyroid, my eyes, and into the organ of my skin. Daily I confess that by His healing whips I am healed in spirit, mind, emotions, and in my physical body too (Isa. 53:4-5).

Guillain-Barre Syndrome (GBS)

See page 221 under "Neurological Disorders."

Hashimoto's Thyroiditis

Prayer of Faith

By the authority of Jesus given to those who believe and follow after Him, I pray with words of faith and command this spirit of death against you and your thyroid gland to leave your body at once! I renounce this label of Hashimoto's thyroiditis and the wicked power behind it. I curse the confusion in your immune system and command order to take over the disorder and that it no longer attacks your healthy tissue, but protects these tissues in your thyroid gland. I renounce the inflammation of this gland; I command it to be gone and not to return. I declare life and healing over your thyroid and that it functions perfectly normally, secreting hormones that influence the chemical reactions throughout your body. I call out commands of faith—energy return, metabolism be strong, reproductive health be healed, and digestion be cleansed and function perfectly normally. In the name of the Lord, I pray in faith, amen.

Confession of Faith

I believe in the power of the blood to deliver me from this spirit of death against my thyroid gland, and from this spirit of confusion misdirecting my immune system, and to heal me of Hashimoto's thyroiditis. I stand firm in the faith that the power of God has reset my immune system and it is on the right course of healing and no longer attacking the tissue of my thyroid gland. My thyroid is no longer weak, but re-created, and functions to perfection. All inflammation of this gland is forever gone, never to return. My thyroid gland is full of life and correctly secrets hormones that influence the chemical reactions throughout my body. I call out commands of faith over my body—I have the energy I need for every day. My metabolism is strong, my reproductive health is healed, and my digestive system is clean and functions perfectly normally. In the name of the Lord, my Healer, I declare in faith, amen.

Inflammatory Bowel Disease (IBD)/ Crohn's Disease and Ulcerative Colitis

Prayer of Faith

In the name of Jesus your Healer, I renounce this attack from a spirit of death, IBD, immune system malfunction, and inflammation that is causing injury to the bowel. Humans may not understand this disease fully, but your Creator Jesus does, and it is upon His wisdom we call during this time of need in your life.

I renounce generational bondage to this curse that has come upon you and is hurting you from the inside to the outside. By the authority of Christ given to His people (Luke 10:19), I command this internal warfare to come to a screeching halt!

For those of you who are suffering from Crohn's disease, I release the healing power of the Lord to flow through the deep layers of your digestive tract, to heal its lining from inflammation and the small and even large intestines from injury.

And for those who suffer from ulcerative colitis, I release this same healing power into the lining of your large intestine, your colon, and rectum to heal them of all inflammation and ulcers.

I pray this in faith over you that you are delivered from the daily worry and suffering that you have been going through, and that diarrhea, rectal bleeding, abdominal pain, fatigue, and weight loss come to an end, in Jesus' name I pray, amen.

Confession of Faith

Even while in this battle, I still believe in the healing power of the Lord, and I declare that no weapon formed against me will prosper (Isa. 54:17). I take comfort in knowing that when I feel weak, He remains strong within me (2 Cor. 12:10) and that by His stripes I am healed! (Isa. 53:5).

With words of faith, I declare that I am delivered and set free from IBD, Crohn's, and ulcerative colitis, and that my entire digestive tract is re-created, healed, strengthened, fully functional, and made whole for the glory of the Lord. All internal warfare within my body is done away with, at peace, and I can eat healthy food to nourish my body without pain and suffering. I do not struggle with anemia, for God is my Healer and gives strength to my body. I do not have to fear daily activities, for God is with me, and I declare His healing power over my body, in Jesus' name, amen.

Multiple Sclerosis

Prayer of Faith

I pray for you, standing in faith, believing that the promises of healing found throughout the Word of God are received into your physical body and that you are delivered and healed from this spirit of death, MS, and this autoimmune disease. I speak life, re-creation, health, and strength into your brain, spinal cord, central nervous system, into your immune system, and to the protective sheaths (myelin) covering your nerve fibers and throughout the communication system between your brain and the rest of your body. I pray that you will choose to reject all hopeless medical reports and lying symptoms that the enemy the devil is trying to put on you. I pray that you arise above this wicked attack of satan and activate your faith, speak faith-filled words, and act like you will live to a ripe old age for the glory of your Lord. I stand in faith with you, amen.

Confession of Faith

In the name of the living God, Jesus Christ, I renounce this spirit of death, MS, and autoimmune disease. I curse this power of death over my brain and spinal cord and a spirit of confusion attacking my immune system. I have a blood covenant with the Father through the blood of Jesus that gives me the spiritual right to a strong and healthy brain, spinal cord, and central nervous system. I will not back down or give in to a spirit of fear that I will be or will remain disabled. This is not the work of Christ, and I do not accept this hopeless medical report or these lying symptoms trying to get me to give up on life. No, I am not entering into the valley of the shadow of death. I choose life, and I choose to live strong and healthy and act as though I am alive and well.

I speak creative miracles into my immune system and declare that it will heal my body and not attack it. I speak re-creation to the protective sheath (myelin) that covers my nerve fibers. My nerve fibers are refreshed, and the communication between my brain and the rest of my body is restored. My body receives my re-created brain signals and obeys God's promises of healing and restoration. I live to testify of the goodness of the Lord in a re-created body that is full of His strength and healing power. This I declare forever, amen.

Myasthenia Gravis Disease

Prayer of Faith

By faith in the redemptive power of the blood of Jesus, I stand in faith with you that no weapon formed against you will prosper (Isa. 54:17). This spirit of death, myasthenia gravis disease, is a weapon of warfare from the devil himself against you, but I firmly demand satan to back off. He will not have his way with you. All the damage that he has caused, muscle weakness and fatigue, and the voluntary control of your muscles that he has stolen from you we take back by faith, by all the authority Jesus gave to us over that fallen angel and his demonic force. By the power in the name of Jesus, devil, you bow in defeat. For what our Lord Jesus says, we say, and we agree with His healing promises in Isaiah 53:4-5 that by His stripes the one in need here is healed.

I declare words of faith that your immune system is healed and no longer attacks your God-given ability to control your muscles. They are full of strength, delivered from weakness and fatigue. Your leg and arm muscles are strong; your eyelids no longer droop but can stay wide open; you do not have double vision but normal vision; there is no difficulty with speaking, chewing, swallowing, or breathing. For your Creator Jesus has healed and made you whole for a testimony in these latter days of a loving God who is alive and well and wills the same for all people, amen and amen.

Confession of Faith

Jesus, by the power of Your redemptive blood I begin to confess now and every day that You are Lord over me and You have delivered me from this spirit of death, myasthenia gravis disease, and from a spirit of confusion over my immune system. I declare words of faith over my body—that I am delivered and healed from them. They are not mine, for You, Father God, are the giver of good gifts, and these are not good but evil. Therefore, they are from the devil, and I do not receive anything from that fallen foe or from his demonic force. For by the grace of God I am healed; I am made whole.

By faith in the name and by the power of Your precious blood, I declare what You have already given to me—a healthy and well-operating immune system that supplies my muscles with strength and energy. My leg and arm muscles are empowered by the redemptive blood of the Lamb of God. My eyelids no longer droop but can stay wide open. I do not have double vision but see clearly. I do not accept difficulty with speaking, chewing, swallowing, or breathing, but I do these things without even thinking about them any longer.

Jesus, You are my creator and the Healer of my body. When I am weak, You remain strong and faithful to me. And I live to testify of Your goodness to all people in these latter days, amen.

PANS/PANDAS: Autoimmune Brain Inflammation

Prayer of Faith

In the mighty name of your deliverer and Healer, Jesus Christ, I stand in the gap for your creative miracle to manifest. I renounce this spirit of death, the source of both PANS and PANDAS, which has come against your life, health, and wellbeing. I release God's miracle-working power into your immune system and into your brain. I declare by faith that your immune system is re-created and functions perfectly normally. No longer does it harm your body but heals your body. The confusion with the antibodies stops and no longer mistakes healthy cells for strep infection or other types of infection. They do what they are created to do, which is to fight the bacteria caused by strep and other infections. Neither can these antibodies affect the tissues in your brain but heal and strengthen them. By spoken words of faith, I build a supernatural wall of protection between the power and physical and psychological symptoms behind these labels and the God-given basal ganglia function. The basal ganglia function is healed and serves you well all the days of your life. All negative and demonic attacks against your psychological and neurological system are healed, and abnormal behaviors such as tics and obsessive-compulsive behaviors be healed in Jesus' name, amen.

Confession of Faith

In Jesus' name, I am healed from PANS/PANDAS. My immune system heals my body and does not harm it. I no longer make ticking noises or act out in obsessive or compulsive ways. My mind and emotions are at peace. I am healed from this disease in Jesus' name, amen.

Pernicious Anemia

Prayer of Faith

I stand in faith with you believing that you are delivered from a spirit of death, this weakness in your immune system, and this vitamin deficiency anemia in Jesus' name. I release the creative and miracle-working power of the Lord to restore healthy red blood cells, intrinsic factor, Vitamin B12, and folate to your body. There is no shortage of these necessary things in heaven, and your body has no lack of them either. I declare what Jesus Christ provided us with already—healing and strength to your body. By faith, your body has an immune system that heals and does not harm the cells in your stomach. These cells can and do produce the right amount of intrinsic factor, and your intestines can and do absorb vitamin B12. I believe with you for all of this, including your bodily function to produce red blood cells that are not too large, just the right size, and they function to perfection, amen.

Confession of Faith

I confess with words of faith that I am delivered from a spirit of death, a confused immune system, and vitamin deficiency anemia in the name of the Lord and Healer, Jesus Christ. By faith, I believe He has restored my healthy red blood cells, intrinsic factor, Vitamin B12, and folate in my body. I do not possess a spirit of lack and have no shortage in me of these necessary things within my body either. I declare what Jesus Christ provides me with already—healing and strength to my body. By faith, my body has an immune system that heals and does not harm the cells in my stomach. These cells can and do produce the right amount of intrinsic factor, and my intestines can and do absorb vitamin B12. I trust in the healing power of my God for all of this, including my bodily function to produce red blood cells that are not too large, just the right size, and they function to perfection, amen.

Psoriasis/Psoriatic Arthritis

Prayer of Faith

My Father in heaven, I pray in faith in the name Your Son, my Savior Jesus. I renounce this autoimmune disorder that causes your skin cells to grow too fast. I speak order to this physical disorder and command that the immune system heals and the natural process of the growth of your skin cells slows down to a normal pace. You are delivered and healed from this curse and the symptoms that come with this label of psoriasis.

I also rebuke this generational curse of psoriatic arthritis and command the root of this issue out of your body. I declare that this negative lineage is broken. We voice-activate with our words of faith deliverance and freedom from this wretched disease. I plead the power of the blood of Jesus over your nails and joints. I command the painful swelling in your fingers and toes, your ligaments and tendons where they meet the joint, and the pain in your back to subside and to stay away. I declare words of faith that you are delivered and healed from psoriatic arthritis, pain-free with full mobility for the glory of the Lord, amen.

Confession of Faith

With my own voice, I declare that I am delivered and healed from psoriasis and psoriatic arthritis. I do not accept this generational curse, for I know the Word of the Lord that I have been delivered from the curse and healed from all disease when Jesus hung on that tree (Gal. 3:13). I speak to my immune system to come under the creative and miracle-working order of my Creator, Jesus. I command my immune system and make no exceptions that you heal my body and do not work overtime to harm my body. I insist that you bow to the name of Jesus and be healed. I declare what I have spiritually from my Father God by the atoning blood of Jesus in Isaiah 53:4-5—healing from all sickness and disease. Because I believe, I receive a new immune system that functions perfectly normally, my skin cells grow at a normal pace, my nails are re-created and they do not crumble and fall apart, but they

All scar tissue in your lungs disappears, and they are able to breathe and tolerate exercise. By the wounds that Jesus bore for you, you are healed and made whole (1 Pet. 2:24). Amen.

Confession of Faith

In the name of the Lord Jesus Christ, I fight the good fight of faith (1 Tim. 6:12) and I am more than a conqueror (Rom. 8:37). I will not die prematurely but live and glorify the works of the Lord (Ps. 118:17). I am created in the mirror image of God and obey His command to subdue the earth and have dominion over every living thing, including sickness and disease (Gen. 1: 26-28). With the power of death and life in my words (Prov. 18:21), I wage war against the very seed of this disease fighting against me. You will not live in me! With this same supernatural power I speak life to my cells, tissues, organs, and systems. I call things that are not as though they already were (Rom. 4:17). I am delivered from premature death, and I am healed from scleroderma. My immune system is re-created, and it heals and does not harm me; it protects and does not attack my connective tissues, including my skin. There is no overproduction or accumulation of collagen in my body tissues. All scar tissue in my lungs disappears, and they can breathe and tolerate exercise. My body functions are in harmony with the Word of God, and by His stripes I am healed and made whole (Isa. 53:4-5). Amen!

Sjögren's Syndrome

Prayer of Faith

By the power of the blood and the name of Jesus, I renounce this nasty work of the enemy, Sjogren's syndrome, the autoimmune disorder of dry eyes and a dry mouth and the open door to attacks against your joints, thyroid, kidneys, liver, lungs, skin, and nerves, and connections to other diseases—rheumatoid arthritis and lupus. Regardless of the negative medical reports, I stand in faith with you for a supernatural healing touch from our Lord.

Romans 4:17 instructs us to call those things which do not exist as though they did, and so I do this for you in the name of Jehovah Rapha, the God who heals. I call forth by faith re-created mucous membranes and moisture-secreting glands of your eyes and mouth; your eyes produce tears and your mouth the much-needed saliva.

I declare by faith that your joints are healed and free from pain, swelling, and stiffness. Your salivary glands are healed as well and are no longer swollen. Your organ of the skin is refreshed by the healing power of the Lord, and it is no longer plagued with rashes or dryness. If you are a woman, you are free from the irritation of vaginal dryness. I come against that persistent dry cough and command it to be healed; you are energized and no longer fatigued. I declare that as you wait upon the Lord, your strength will be renewed; you shall mount up with wings like the eagles. You shall run and not grow weary; you shall walk and not faint for the glory of the Lord rests upon you. In His name I pray this over you, amen.

Confession of Faith

In the name of the Lord my God, Creator of my being, I renounce this spirit of death and its attack against me with Sjogren's syndrome, the autoimmune disorder of dry eyes and a dry mouth and the open door to attacks against my joints, thyroid, kidneys, liver, lungs, skin, and nerves and connections to other diseases—rheumatoid arthritis and lupus. Regardless of the negative medical reports, I stand in faith believing that by the redemptive power of the blood I am healed and made whole.

I declare by faith things that are not as though they already were (Rom. 4:17). So yes, I call forth by faith re-created mucous membranes and moisture-secreting glands of my eyes and mouth, and my eyes produce tears, and my mouth much-needed saliva.

I declare by faith that my joints are healed and free from pain, swelling, and stiffness. My salivary glands are healed as well and are no longer swollen. My skin is refreshed by the healing power of the Lord and is no longer plagued with rashes or dryness. (If you are a woman add this: "I am free from the irritation of vaginal dryness.) I come against a persistent dry cough and command it to be healed; I am no longer fatigued but energized. I declare that as I wait upon my Lord, my strength is renewed; I shall mount up with wings like the eagles. I will run and not grow weary or hurt, I shall walk and not faint for the glory of the Lord rests upon me and strengthens me from day to day. Amen.

Systemic Lupus Erythematosus

Prayer of Faith

In the name of Jehovah Rapha, our Healer, Jesus Christ, I renounce this spirit of death, lupus, this autoimmune disease attacking your body, even the facial rash associated with this disease. I plead the power of the blood of the Lord over your immune system, kidneys, brain, and central nervous system; your blood and blood vessels; and your heart and lungs. I renounce the confusion in your immune system and command it to realign itself with the Word of God that says, *"By*

His stripes you are healed" (Isa. 53.5) so that it heals and does not destroy the body. I speak strength to your kidneys and declare words of faith over them that they are not and will not be diseased or fail you. To your brain and central nervous system, I say you be re-created and function in a normal and healthy manner, and the blood of the Lamb overrides all negative reports against you. I speak to your blood to be re-created with a healthy amount of red blood cells. I declare that you are not sickly because of anemia, but that your blood is fortified by the power of the blood of Christ running through your blood vessels. I add to this words of faith concerning your blood vessels that all swelling be gone for God's great glory. I renounce the inflammation attacking the chest cavity lining— you can breathe free and with ease. I plead God's protection over your lungs that they will not bleed or be susceptible to pneumonia, but they are cleansed by God's healing power. I also renounce inflammation of your heart muscle and arteries. I curse all weakness to cardiovascular disease and heart attacks in Jesus' name, I pray, amen.

Confession of Faith

By faith, I proclaim that the goodness of God to heal is manifesting within and throughout my body. I declare by faith that I am delivered from this spirit of death and the autoimmune disease lupus that has attacked my physical body. With all the authority of Christ given to me (Luke 10:19), I command my immune system to heal and not to harm me, and that my kidneys, brain, and central nervous system; blood and blood vessels; and my heart and lungs all line up to the redemptive promise of healing in God's Word (Isa. 53:4-5). I reject a spirit of fear from negative medical reports. I do not accept kidney disease or their failure, but instead I declare that they are strong and healthy, able to do what they are created to do for my good health and wellbeing. My brain and central nervous system are protected by God from headaches, dizziness, behavioral changes, vision problems, and especially from strokes and seizures. My blood receives a supernatural blood transfusion by faith in the power of my Savior's blood. My blood is healthy, not anemic. I am protected from the risk of bleeding and blood clotting. My blood vessels do not surrender to inflammation but are healed in the name that is above every name—Jesus. My lungs are delivered from this same attack of inflammation, and I can breathe free and easy. They are protected from bleeding and pneumonia. My heart is also protected from disease and this inflammation. My heart muscle and my arteries are strong and full of health. I will not accept negative reports of cardiovascular disease or heart attacks. My Creator Jesus made me strong and healthy, and I will not allow the enemy to steal this gift from me. If he has stolen my health and strength from me, I demand he leave me and get out of the way of God's healing promise to me, amen!

Type 1 Autoimmune Hepatitis

Prayer of Faith

In Jesus' name, I stand in faith on your behalf without wavering (James 1:6) that you are delivered from this spirit of death and healed from this disease, type 1 autoimmune hepatitis. I activate the power of life in my words and declare that your immune system is healed and stops attacking the cells of your liver, and all inflammation and scarring are done away with for the glory of the Lord and for your health and wellbeing, amen.

Confession of Faith

In the name of Jesus, I renounce this disease, autoimmune hepatitis, which is targeting the cells of my liver to harm them. I release the healing virtue of the Lord to flow through my immune system to rid my liver from inflammation and scarring. I command my liver to align itself with God's Word that declares, *"By His stripes I am healed!"* (Isa. 53:4-5). Amen.

Type 1 Diabetes

Prayer of Faith

In the name of Jesus, I intercede for you with prophetic words that can deliver and heal you from type 1 diabetes. Your Creator is God, and He did not design your body with a sick pancreas that cannot produce the daily amount of insulin your body needs. So I pray according to the Word that by His stripes you are healed (Isa. 53:5) and delivered from this disease. I speak creative words (Gen. 1) that bring forth a strong and healthy pancreas that puts forth a sufficient supply of insulin into your bloodstream, that allows sugar to enter your cells, and permits your natural insulin to lower the amount of sugar in your bloodstream. As your blood sugar level drops, your pancreas puts less insulin into the bloodstream. I believe that the healing power of our Lord is working in you, amen.

Confession of Faith

In the mighty name of Jesus, type 1 diabetes is not greater in power than my Lord. The medical field deems this as incurable; perhaps for them it is, but nothing is too difficult for my Jesus (Jer. 32:17). I curse this spirit of death and this genetic curse attacking my immune system, my pancreas, my islet cells, and my natural supply of insulin. I say to the devil, "Get out of my body!" I have been redeemed from the curse when Jesus hung on that Cross (Gal. 3:13). I will not accept this disease any longer in my body, for I have been redeemed by the blood of the Lamb (Eph. 1:7). By the creative power of the spoken word, I speak into existence a brand-new pancreas into my body, and my islet cells are replenished, and by the grace of God they function perfectly normally and it produces the exact amount of insulin my body needs every day.

Part 2

BLOOD DISORDERS

Acquired Hemophilia

See page 47 under "Autoimmune Disorders."

Anemia

Prayer of Faith

I lift you up to Jesus, the Great Physician, who not only creates your body but knows the intricate workings of it and what needs to happen to undo the havoc the devil has caused in it. So with His creative power of the spoken word (Gen. 1), I voice-activate faith for your healing; with the power of life and death in the tongue (Prov. 18:21) I renounce this blood disorder, anemia. I release Messiah's healing power into your red blood cells and command them to multiply to the correct number or volume and declare by faith that there is no lack of hemoglobin found within them. The notable signs of this creative miracle come forth—your skin, mucous membranes, and nail beds are a healthy color, and your tissues receive the proper amount of oxygen. Pulsating noises in your ears, dizziness, fainting, and shortness of breath stop in Jesus' name. The size of your heart returns to normal, and a rapid pulse slows down to a normal rate. All this I pray in faith for your health and wellbeing, amen.

Confession of Faith

I believe in the creative, miracle-working power of my Great Physician, Jesus. He made my body, and He knows how to fix it when the enemy harms it. I believe in the power of the spoken word (Gen. 1) and in the power of life and death in my words (Prov. 18:21). In Messiah's name, I renounce this blood disorder and command it to come under the perfect order of God so that my red blood cells multiply to the correct number and volume. I declare by faith that there is no lack of hemoglobin found within them. I declare by faith in the healing power of the atonement that the notable signs of this miracle come forth—my skin, mucous membranes, and nail beds are a healthy color, and my tissues receive the proper amount of oxygen. The pulsating noises in my ears, dizziness, shortness of breath, and fainting stop in Jesus' name. My heart is restored to a healthy size, and my pulse slows down to a normal rate. By faith in the blood of Jesus, I am healed and made whole, amen.

Hemophilia

Prayer of Faith

I am confident as I stand before His throne of grace on your behalf (Heb. 4:16) that we serve a God of healing (Exod. 15:26). I stand with you on this foundation of faith (Heb. 11:1) that you are healed from this bleeding disorder and made whole by His blood that He shed for you at the whipping post

(Isa. 53:4-5). I declare with the power of spoken words (Rom. 4:17) that you do not have hemophilia, and you have an ample daily supply of clotting factors that seal up your wounds. In Jesus' name I confidently pray in faith, amen.

Confession of Faith

I believe in the healing process of the Lord. I first believe and then I see it manifest (Gen. 1), and because I do believe without wavering (Heb. 10:23) I am confident that as I stand before His throne of grace (Heb. 4:16) I am healed in Jesus' name (Ps. 30:2). I make a bold statement of faith that I am delivered from this bleeding disorder. I do not accept this generational curse, for I have a rich inheritance from God that includes my healing from hemophilia (Ps. 103:2-3). Abba Father has no lack of heavenly supply of clotting factors, so by faith I receive my daily amount that my body has need of to seal up any wounds. By His stripes I am healed and made whole (Isa. 53:4-5)! Amen.

Sepsis

Prayer of Faith

I plead the power of the blood of Jesus over you. I declare words of faith that you will not die but live and declare the works of the Lord (Ps. 118:17). You have been redeemed from this blood poisoning curse, sepsis, when Jesus became the curse for you (Gal. 3:13). I declare words of life (Prov. 18:21) that your body is healed from all types of infections, your immune system is strengthened by the power of the Spirit (Zech. 4:6), all inflammation is gone, and tissue damage and organ failure is healed. In Jesus' name, I pray in faith for you, amen.

Confession of Faith

I declare the Word of the Lord over myself: I will not die but live and declare the works of the Lord (Ps. 118:17). I am redeemed from this blood poisoning curse, sepsis, when Jesus became the curse for me (Gal. 3:13). By His healing stripes (Isa. 53:4-5) my immune system is strengthened, all inflammation is gone, tissue damage and organ failure is healed in Jesus' name, amen.

Sickle Cell Disease and Sickle Cell Retinopathy

Prayer of Faith

In the name of Jesus, I renounce this spirit of death and sickle cell disease. I curse this generational curse and the disorder in your red blood cells. I release the healing and creative power of the Lord Jesus Christ to restore order in your red blood cells, to re-form the shape of your red blood cells from sickle shapes to round shapes as they should be. They are soft and not sticky, and they can travel through your small blood vessels and not get stuck or clog the blood flow, and they carry the much-needed oxygen to all parts of your body. I declare that your hemoglobin is not abnormal but normal, and there is no shortage of red blood cells, because Almighty God does not have a shortage of red blood cells to supply your body with. I decree a wall of protection between you and infections, acute chest syndrome, and strokes. I declare that you will live free and healed from sickle cell disease and sickle cell retinopathy and fulfill your days for the glory of the Lord, amen and amen.

Confession of Faith

By the power of the blood of Jesus, I am delivered from this generational curse of sickle cell disease. I declare words of faith, and there is no disorder in my red blood cells, and they are re-formed from sickle shapes to round shapes. They are soft and not sticky and can travel with ease throughout my small blood vessels and not get stuck or clog my blood flow. They carry the much-needed oxygen to all parts of my body. I raise up the standard of the blood of Christ in my life and prophesy that my hemoglobin is normal, and I have no shortage of red blood cells. I hold up my shield of faith against the wiles of the enemy against me, and I spiritually construct a wall of protection between me and infections, acute chest syndrome, and strokes. Sickle cell disease, you do not control me. With all the authority Jesus Christ gave to me, I command you out, and take your sidekick sickle cell retinopathy with you. In Jesus' name, I am healed, I am delivered, and I am free from your power, amen.

Von Willebrand Factor

Prayer of Faith

In the name of our great God, Almighty Jesus, I stand against this spirit of death and blood disorder, Von Willebrand factor. I believe in the release of this creative, miracle-working power of the Lord to supernaturally re-create your body's daily supply of this sticky substance, Von Willebrand factor, which allows your platelets to stick together and form clots. In Jesus' name I declare what you already have—healing (Isa. 53:4-5) in the reputation of His good name (Prov. 22:1), amen.

Confession of Faith

In the name of Jesus, I declare what I already have—a supernatural supply of Von Willebrand factor. There is no shortage of this sticky substance in the supply rooms of heaven, and neither is there a shortage in my body. My body produces its proper daily amount because I dare to activate my faith in the power of the redemptive blood of Jesus, and because I have no shortage of Von Willebrand factor, my platelets can do their job and stick together to form clots. In His healing power I believe without wavering (James 1:6) in the reputation of His good name (Prov. 22:1) and receive my healing, amen.

Part 3

BRAIN DISORDERS

ADHD/ADD

Inattentive ADHD, also known as ADD (Attention Deficit Disorder)

Prayer of Faith

In the name of Jesus, I renounce this label of inattentive ADHD and its negative manifestation of the inability to focus. This is not a gift from God, but an attack of the devil, and I send it back to where it came from, the pit of hell. I declare words of faith that produce creative miracles within your brain and central nervous system. Your mind and emotions are at peace, and you can do as Philippians 4:13 says you can do—all things through Christ who strengthens you, including the ability to concentrate and focus. For the glory of God and for your well-being I pray and believe for you and with you, amen.

Confession of Faith

Through Christ, I can do all things (Phil. 4:13) including the ability to concentrate and focus. By faith in the power of the Cross, I am delivered and healed from spiritual and physical manifestations of inattentive ADHD. I declare words of faith over myself—my brain is re-created, I am not easily distracted, and I can pay attention for long periods of time. In Him, my weakness has become my strength, and concentration and focus have become my forte in Jesus' name, amen.

Hyperactive/Impulsive ADHD

Prayer of Faith

I plead the power of the blood of Jesus over your mind, emotions, behaviors, physical brain, and your central nervous system. I renounce this label and the power behind it, hyperactive/impulsive ADHD, which has been placed upon you. I only accept the word of the Lord concerning this matter: by His healing whips (Isa. 53:4-5) you are healed and delivered in spirit, soul (mind and emotions), and physical body. Faith is the only evidence necessary for God's remedy (Heb. 11:1). When Jesus became the curse (Gal. 3:13), He broke the binding chains of this and any generational seed passed on to you. By faith we activate this bondage-breaking power.

By His Spirit and not by your might or power (Zech. 4:6), you can sit still and act appropriately, pay attention for long periods of time, learn to control excessive talking, allow others to speak without interrupting, and exercise the fruit of the spirit of patience in Jesus' name, amen.

Confession of Faith

By faith in the redemptive power of the Cross, I believe that I am delivered from this label of hyperactive/impulsive ADHD (Isa. 53:4-5) and that Jesus broke this binding chain that has been wrapped around me and the seed of this that may have been passed on to me from past generations. This is not a good gift from God, so I send it back to enemy from whence it came. Jesus became my curse-breaker when He hung upon that tree (Gal. 3:13), and because of Him I am free (Gal. 5:1).

No matter what the world says, I believe there is hope for me, and according to God's Word my faith is the only evidence I need (Heb. 11:1). I choose to hold on to this confession of faith without wavering (James 1:6): that my mind and emotions, my ability to control my behaviors, and my physical brain and central nervous system are healed. By His Spirit and not by my might or power (Zech. 4:6) I can sit still and act appropriately, pay attention for long periods of time, learn to control excessive talking, allow others to speak without interrupting, and exercise the fruit of the spirit of patience. In Jesus' name, I am free, amen.

Combined ADHD

Prayer of Faith

By faith, I claim the healing power of Jehovah Rapha, our God who heals you from this label of combined ADHD. This disease does not come from God, we do not accept it, we send it back to the sender, the devil. By the healing power of the blood of Jesus Christ, your mind, emotions, and behaviors, along with your physical brain and central nervous system, are healed and made whole. Jesus is your curse-breaker (Gal.

3:13). He broke this stronghold over you, and we activate this power by faith in His work at Calvary.

By the amazing power of the blood of Jesus, your mind and emotions, your ability to control your behaviors, your physical brain and central nervous system have all received the healing touch of the Lord, and I choose to activate my faith on your behalf in the redemptive power of Calvary for you. In His name I pray in faith, amen.

Confession of Faith

My God who heals me, Jehovah Rapha, has delivered me from the label of combined ADHD and the demonic force behind it. This is not a gift from God, I do not accept it, and I return it to its rightful owner, the devil. By the all-powerful blood of Christ, my mind and emotions, my ability to control my behaviors, my physical brain and central nervous system have all received the healing touch of the Lord, and I choose to activate my faith daily in the redemptive power of Calvary over me.

By His Spirit and not by my might or power (Zech. 4:6), I can sit still and act appropriately. I am not easily distracted but can pay close attention for long periods of time, learn to control excessive talking, allow others to speak without interrupting, and exercise the fruits of the spirit of self-control and patience. I add to this declaration of faith that this weakness has been transformed by His redemptive power, and these areas that were once weak have been healed and have become my strengths, in Jesus' name, amen.

Autism

Prayer of Faith

For the glory of God and for your wellbeing, I stand in faith believing that you are delivered from this spirit of death, spirit of violence, and this torturous disease called autism. I do not accept that you will be like this for the rest of your life. I believe in the healing power of Jesus Christ, and my Bible speaks truth to all matters. I put my faith in Jehovah Rapha, who heals you in spirit, heals your mind and emotions, and heals your physical body as well. I believe in the power of the re-creation of your brain and that by His healing whips (Isa. 53:4-5) you are healed, your brain is re-created, and by faith I activate this miracle for you and with you. I believe you can look me and others in the eye and stop these repetitive behaviors such as rocking, spinning, and flapping. You no longer harm yourself by banging your head or biting yourself. These tantrums stop now, in Jesus' name! You can learn to speak and to communicate your needs and wants clearly to others. I believe in the power of the bondage-breaker, Jesus, and when He hung on that tree, He broke this curse so you can be free (Gal. 3:15). And yes, I do believe that you are free. Whom Jesus sets free is free indeed (John 8:36). I believe you will learn to do anything you set your mind to do, because you are healed for the glory of God, amen.

Confession of Faith

In the name of Jesus, I am free from autism and all its symptoms. By the power of His strength, I can look you in the eye; I can talk and make reasonable conversation. I can learn to overcome all negative behaviors. I no longer need to rock, spin, or flap my hands. I will no longer throw tantrums, bang my head, or bite myself. I am free from a spirit of death, a spirit of violence, and a spirit of torment. I am free from this label of autism and all its negative reports. I will learn the skills I need to function as a happy and productive citizen. In Jesus' name, I believe, amen.

Blood Clots (Harmful)

Prayer of Faith

In Jesus' name, I curse blood clots forming in your body for no goodreason. I release the healing power of Jesus to flow into these harmful blood clots and supernaturally dissolve and eliminate them from yourbody. With all the authority given to me by Jesus (Luke 10:19), blood clots will not travel to your brain, heart, or lungs. No weapon formed against your health and wellbeing will prosper, including these unwanted blood clots (Isa. 54:17). The Word of God defies every death report spoken or written against your longevity. I decree a supernatural wall of protection between you and death. I declare that you will not die but live and declare the works of the Lord (Ps. 118:17), in the name of the Lord our God, amen.

Confession of Faith

I hold fast the confession of my hope without wavering, for He whopromised is faithful (Heb. 10:23). I will not die but live and declare the works of the Lord (Ps. 118:17). This weapon of harmful blood clots formed against me will not prosper (Isa. 54:17). The Lord will sustain,refresh, and strengthen me (Ps. 41:3), and He will satisfy me with long life (Ps. 91:6). The Lord will preserve me and keep me alive (Ps. 41:2), and with all the authority gifted to me by Christ (Luke 10:19), blood clots will not enter my brain, heart, or lungs. I command that these unwanted blood clots dissolve and be gone from my body supernaturally by the redemptive power of the blood of Jesus Christ and cause me no harm, amen.

Brain Dead

See page 110 under "Death."

Brain Hemorrhage

Prayer of Faith

In the name of the Lord your God, your Healer (Exod. 15:26), I renounce this spirit of death, brain death, brain bleed, lack of oxygen to your brain tissues, brain damage, and organ failure. I release the healing power of the blood of Jesus to restore life to your brain and throughout your every cell, tissue, organ, and system of your body. By faith, I release the breath of Holy Spirit into your being (John 20:22), and I declare words of complete faith in the redemptive work of Christ: you will not die but live (Ps. 118:17), and you will fulfill your God-given destiny full of life, health, and strength (Jer. 29:11). I stand with you and for you when you can't stand against satan and his wicked works opposing you (Eph. 6:11). I remain strong and courageous with you, and we will not give in to fear or discouragement (Josh. 1:9), for greater is our Lord Jesus in us than satan is in this world (1 John 4:4). With the power of life and death in the tongue (Prov. 28:11), I declare by faith that you are healed and made whole (Isa. 53:4-5), amen.

Confession of Faith

In Jesus' name, I renounce this spirit of death fighting against me; I will not die but live (Ps. 118:17). I renounce the effects from brain death, brain bleed, lack of oxygen to my brain

body. I have a great memory; I can pay attention, stay focused, concentrate, and process the information that comes into my brain. I am great with reasoning and problem-solving, and I have good judgment skills. I am not jittery or hyperactive, and I have control over my mind and emotions. I am at peace with Jesus and with myself in Jesus' name, amen.

Strokes

Prayer of Faith

In the name of Jesus your Healer, I stand in the gap for you, being strong in the faith that with Jesus all things are possible (Mark 10:27). I renounce this violent attack from the spirit of death. I release the healing power of the blood of the Lamb of God to flow through your entire brain to re-create and make it whole. I declare by faith that you will not die but live and declare the glory of the Lord (Ps. 118:17).

I renounce the spiritual chains of paralysis and declare that you are loosed (Luke 13:12), that you can stand, bend, walk, run, jump, and even dance if you want to. You can speak with clarity and understand what others are saying and freely join in conversations with others. You can read and write too. I believe that your memory is restored and that you can reason, make judgments, and understand concepts.

I renounce a spirit of depression and command it to leave you now. I believe in the power of supernatural joy and that this is God's strength for you (Neh. 8:10). Laughter is God's medicine, and you can laugh and find the joy in each day (Prov. 17:22).

I thank the Lord that you are alive today. In His precious name, amen.

Confession of Faith

I declare by faith that no weapon formed against me shall prosper (Isa. 54:17). I will not die but live and declare the glorious work of the Lord in my life (Ps. 118:17). With words of faith, I speak life into my every, cell, tissue, organ, and system. My strength is renewed like that of the eagle; I will run and not grow weary, and I will walk and not faint (Isa. 40:31). I am loosed from the bondage of this stroke (Luke 13:12). I choose not to grieve or to be depressed, for the joy of the Lord is my strength and stronghold (Neh. 8:10). I believe and trust in the Lord my God that I have been delivered from a spirit of death and the effects of this stroke and that this healing belongs to me (Ps. 103:2-3) in Jesus' name, amen.

Traumatic Brain Injury

Prayer of Faith

By faith in the resurrection power that raised Christ from the dead (Rom. 8:11), I renounce this spirit of death from this traumatic brain injury. I release the healing power of Jesus to flow through your every cell, tissue, organ, and system of your body, and all injuries to your brain be healed and re-created with your brain functions restored. I declare that you will not die but live and declare the works of the Lord (Ps. 118:17). I stand in faith in the redemptive power of the blood of Jesus that heals you (Isa. 53:4-5), amen.

Confession of Faith

I will not die but live (Ps. 118:17), and by my faith in the blood of Jesus shed for me I am healed and made whole (Isa. 53:4-5). By that same spirit that raised Jesus from the dead (Rom. 8:11), I am raised up out of this bed, out of this chair, able to function and to remember and to fulfill my destiny in Christ, amen.

Part 4

CANCERS

All Types of Cancer

Prayer of Faith

In the name of Jesus Christ your Healer, I renounce this spirit of death, all cancer, cancerous cells, and tumors. With all the authority that Jesus gave to us, I command these cancerous cells and tumors to die off at their seed, to shrivel and dry up at their roots, and to be supernaturally gone. I decree a wall of protection between your life and them. I declare the Word of the Lord over you: that your cells, tissues, organs, and systems are cleansed, healed, strengthened, re-created, and made whole, cancer-free, and cancer-proof. I align my faith with the Word of the Lord that declares you will not die but live and declare the works of the Lord (Ps. 118:17). In His most gracious name, I pray, amen.

Confession of Faith

For the glory of the Lord, I confess daily that I will not die prematurely, but I will live (Ps. 118:17). I boldly declare that my every cell, tissue, organ, and system in my body is cleansed, delivered, healed, re-created, strengthened, and made whole, cancer-free, and cancer-proof. I believe in the living God, who is both able and willing to heal (Luke 5:12-13) all who come to Him (Matt. 15:29-31). I believe that with Him all things are possible (Mark 10:27), and greater is He (Jesus) who is in me than he (the devil) that is in this world (1 John 4:4). Even when I walk through the darkest valley, I will not be afraid, for You are close beside me. Your rod and Your staff protect and comfort me (Ps. 23:4), and by Your stripes (Isa. 53:5), I am healed! Amen.

Bone Cancer

Prayer of Faith

I pray in faith without wavering (Heb. 10:23) over the health and wellbeing of your bones. By the power of life and death in the tongue (Prov. 18:21), I command cancer, cancerous cells, and tumors to die at the very seed and root and to be supernaturally eliminated from your body. I decree a wall of protection between the workings of this spirit of death and your bones and the rest of your body. I declare by faith what you already have from the Lord: the healing of your bones (Isa. 53:4-5). I proclaim words of faith that your bones, the cells and tissues of your bones, and the cartilage between your bones are cancer-free, cancer-proof, pain-free, strong, and healthy, and they defy every negative report! In Jesus' name, you are healed, amen.

Confession of Faith

In Jesus' name, I believe, and I do not waver in the faith (Heb. 10:23) that by His healing whips (Isa. 53:4-5) my bones, the cells and tissues within my bones, and my cartilage between my joints are cancer-free, cancer-proof, pain-free, and healed. The life of God flows through them, and they are strong by the power of His Spirit (Zech. 4:6). I obey the Word of God and call things that are not as though they already exist (Rom. 4:17). I am free from cancerous cells and tumors. I am loosed from this infirmity of cancer (Luke 12:13). I will not die but live and declare the works of the Lord (Ps. 118:17), amen.

Brain Cancer

Prayer of Faith

I pray in faith to Jehovah Rapha, the God who heals you (Exod. 15:26). I renounce this spirit of death, brain cancer, cancer cells, tumors, and the confusion taking place within the DNA of your brain cells. I speak creative miracles into the DNA of your brain cells, that they align themselves to God's perfect design, their God-given life cycle, and that they live and die appropriately. They help your brain and do not cause it harm. I speak death to the very center of all cancerous cells and tumors and command them to die off and be supernaturally eliminated from your body. This cancer will not travel to other parts of your body. You be delivered from the spirit of death; healed from cancer, cancerous cells, and tumors; and filled with life and life in abundance (John 10:10). I declare that you will not die but live and declare the works of the Lord (Ps. 118:17), in Jesus' name, amen.

Confession of Faith

Lord God, I judge You faithful (Heb. 11:11) to redeem me from this curse of the enemy (Gal. 3:13). You are my refuge in times of trouble (Ps. 9:9-10), and my peace comes from You

(John 16:33). You are the Lord who heals me (Exod. 15:26). You took this infirmity and bore this sickness (Matt. 8:17).

I take a strong stance of faith, and I command in the name of Jesus that these tumors in my brain die off at the seed, dry up at the roots, and be supernaturally eliminated from my body. With all the authority of Christ that has been given to me (Luke 10:19), I demand, without exception, that the DNA in my brain cells lines up to God's perfect design, and they do not override their life cycle, but they live and die as they are supposed to. They do not over-multiply and form tumors, and they do not metastasize to other parts of my body. No, they submit to my command, for God has given me dominion over every living thing that moves on this earth, and this includes the DNA within my cells (Gen. 1:26-28).

With the creative power of my words (Gen. 1), I speak healing, strength, and creative miracles throughout my brain. All brain damage be healed and brain functions restored; where death has occurred, I receive resurrection life. I declare that I will not die but live and declare the work of the Lord (Ps. 118:17). With these words I confess over myself, amen.

Breast Cancer

See page 133 under "Female Disorders."

Cervical Cancer

See page 134 under "Female Disorders."

Colon Cancer/Colorectal Cancer

Prayer of Faith

I pray in the mighty name of Jesus and by the power of His redemptive blood to deliver and heal you from a spirit of death, colon and rectal cancers, cancerous cells, polyps, and tumors. I renounce these cancerous labels and the destructive power behind them. I release by faith the healing power of the Lord to flow through your large intestine (colon) and rectum to cleanse them from all impurities of death and disease; to supernaturally dissolve all cancerous cells, polyps, and tumors and eliminate them from your body; and cancerous cells will not metastasize to other parts of the body. I declare words of faith that line up with God's Word that declares He will take away all sickness from you (Deut. 7:15), that He will satisfy you with long life (Ps. 91:16), and that the Lord will sustain, refresh, and strengthen you (Ps. 41:3). For your wellbeing and God's great glory I pray this in faith for you, amen.

Confession of Faith

I call upon the name of the Lord and declare by faith that I am delivered from this spirit of death, colon and rectal cancers, cancerous cells, polyps, and tumors. I receive the promise of God's Word that He will take away all sickness from me (Deut. 7:15), and I judge Him faithful to keep His promise to me (Heb. 11:11). I receive His miracle-working power into my colon and rectum and trust that He will cleanse them from all impurities and residue of death and cancer. I accept this healing power of His to supernaturally dissolve all cancerous cells, polyps, and tumors in me and eliminate them from my body. This cancer will not metastasize to other parts of my body. The DNA of my cells fulfills God's original design; they live and die according to His life cycle for them. There is no abnormality found within them, nor do they overproduce, but only create a healthy number of cells every day. I bless the Lord and forget not all of His benefits, who forgives all my iniquities, who heals all my diseases (Ps. 103:2-3). I continue to confess these words full of hope, faith, healing, and strength over my body every day. I dare to believe in the creative, miracle-working power of my Lord to re-create my colon and rectum. In His name, I stand in faith, amen.

Endometrial Cancer

See page 136 under "Female Disorders."

Glioblastoma Multiforme

Prayer of Faith

I lift a prayer of faith up to Abba Father on your behalf against the growth of the seed of these gliomas in your brain cells (astrocytes) that surround the nerve cells in your brain. I renounce this spirit of death moving throughout your brain and/or spinal cord and this cancer causing an uprise against your health and wellbeing. I declare the Word of the living Christ—that you will not die but live (Ps. 118:17). For He has redeemed you from this curse by becoming the curse for you (Gal. 3:13). With the creativity of the spoken word (Gen. 1), I call things that are not as though they already exist (Rom. 4:17). By words of faith, I bring forth the re-creation of the DNA in your cells. They no longer malfunction but function to perfection. They do not overproduce but manufacture the proper number of healthy cells that are both cancer-free and cancer-proof, and they fulfill their proper life cycle. With the power of life and death in the tongue (Prov. 18:21), I release the power of death into these gliomas, their stem cells, the enzyme CDK5 that they produce, and into all cancerous cells and tumors. I curse them from the inside to the outside and command them to be supernaturally eliminated from your body, never to resurrect, come back to life, or to return to your brain and spine again. All brain damage and other negative effects that this has done to you, be healed and made whole again, in Jesus' name, amen.

Confession of Faith

By faith in my Healer Jesus Christ, I confess that I will not die but live (Ps. 118:17). I am loosed from this stronghold of death and cancer (Luke 13:12). With the power of life and death in my words (Prov. 18:21), I speak death and destruction into the seed of these gliomas in my brain cells (astrocytes) that surround the nerve cells in my brain, and into the stem cells of these gliomas, and the enzyme CDK5 that they produce, and into all cancerous cells and tumors. I curse them from the inside to the outside and command them to be supernaturally eliminated from my body, never to resurrect, come back to life, or to return to my brain and spine again. I speak re-creation and resurrection power into my brain and spine. No weapon formed against me will prosper (Isa. 54:17) because I overcome by the blood of the Lamb and by the words of my testimony (Rev. 12:11). I boldly proclaim that I am healed by His stripes (Isa. 53:4-5)! I am cancer-free and cancer-proof for the glory of God, amen.

Leukemia

Prayer of Faith

In Jesus' name, with God nothing is impossible, and neither is this! I renounce this spirit of death and leukemia attacking your body. I release the Spirit of life, the power of Holy Spirit backed by the blood of Jesus, to flow in and throughout the blood-forming tissues, bone marrow, and lymphatic system and to resurrect what is dead, awaken what is dormant, and re-create a normal white blood cell count for you. I speak to every cell, tissue, organ, and system in your body to align itself with the Word of God that declares by His stripes you are healed and made whole, spiritually, mentally, emotionally, and physically. All this we stand together in faith for the glory of the Lord, amen.

Confession of Faith

I declare by faith that my cells, tissues, organs, and systems are aligned to the Word of God that declares I am healed (Isa. 53:4-5). I believe that I am delivered from premature death and from this cancer, leukemia, in Jesus' name. By the power of life and death in my tongue (Prov. 18:21), I speak death to all cancerous cells that are attacking my blood-forming tissues, including my bone marrow and lymphatic system. By the power of His healing blood, they are re-created and function to perfection. By faith in the goodness of my Jesus, the DNA of my blood cells is transformed from abnormal to normal, and my white blood cells, red blood cells, and platelets are normal. By His mercy and grace, my mind and emotions are at peace, for I trust in my Lord's faithfulness to me, amen.

Myeloma

Prayer of Faith

By the power of the blood of Jesus, I renounce this spirit of death and this cancer of the plasma cells. I curse this label of myeloma and the destructive power behind it. I command this accumulation of cancerous plasma cells in the bone marrow to die out, never to return, and make room for a healthy amount of blood cells.

I release the healing power of the Lamb of God who willingly sacrificed Himself for your deliverance from premature death and for the healing of your plasma cells. I speak re-creation of these white blood cells, and by faith they produce antibodies that recognize and attack germs. I renounce all the negative effects against your body. I plead the power of His blood over your plasma cells and antibodies, and I speak peace inside your bones, that they are free from pain. I renounce anemia and declare words of faith that you have healthy red blood cells and they can carry adequate oxygen to your body's tissues. I speak re-creation to your kidneys and that they can do the job they were created to do. I decree a wall of protection between you and infections. All this I speak by faith, believing that He who began a work in you will complete it. In the mighty name I claim this prayer of faith to be true, amen.

Confession of Faith

I dare to believe and confess with my mouth that I am delivered from premature death and healed from this cancer of the plasma cells. I curse this label of myeloma and the destructive force behind it. I command this accumulation of cancerous plasma cells inside my bone marrow to die off immediately, move out never to return, and make room for healthy blood cells that fulfill their life cycle. Cancer cannot metastasize to other parts of my body, in Jesus' name. I believe and receive this healing from my Lord.

I receive His healing power into my body, and I accept from Him re-created plasma cells in healthy amounts, and these white blood cells can produce antibodies that recognize and attack germs. I speak the peace of God deep inside my bones and declare words of faith that they are healed and pain-free. I declare words of faith, "I am not sick with anemia, but I have healthy red blood cells, and they can carry adequate oxygen to my body's tissues." I align my faith with the re-creation of my kidneys; they can do the job they were created to do. I decree a wall of protection between myself and infections. In the mighty name I claim this prayer of faith to be true, and it belongs to me, amen.

Ovarian Cancer

See page 144 under "Female Disorders."

Pancreatic Cancer

Prayer of Faith

I stand in faith believing with you that you have already been redeemed by the power of His blood from premature death, cancer of the pancreas, cancerous cells, and from malfunctioning DNA inside of your pancreas. I declare words of faith that the DNA inside of your pancreas is re-created and your cells function to the perfection of God's design for them. These cells do not over-multiply, but they fulfill God's plan of creation for them—they live and die according to the life cycle God created for them. They abide by this design and no other, the confusion of the DNA of your squamous cells, and the abnormal cells (carcinomas) that divide without control.

I release the healing power of Jesus, the King of kings, to flow into the middle and outer layers of your skin, undoing the damage from ultraviolet radiation from the sun and/or tanning beds and lamps. I align my faith with your faith for the re-creation of your squamous cells, the DNA of these cells, and their function. By faith in the power of the redemptive blood of Christ, they are cleansed and healed and you are made whole, amen.

Confession of Faith

I believe without a shadow of doubt in the healing power of my Lord, Jesus Christ, who is both able and willing to heal all those who come to Him, including me (Luke 5:12-13). As I do right now, with bold faith to restore health to me and to heal me of my wounds (Prov. 4:20-22). I accept His healing power to flow into the middle and outer layers of my skin, undoing the damage from ultraviolet radiation from the sun and/or tanning beds and lamps, to cleanse and re-create my squamous cells, the DNA of these cells, and to deliver them from confusing messages to overproduce squamous cells. I declare order where confusion has been in operation in my cellular realm. I believe by faith that I am cleansed, delivered, and healed from this label and set free from its destructive power, amen and amen.

Melanoma

Prayer of Faith

I believe in the healing power of the Lord to deliver you from this spirit of death, melanoma, attacking your melanocytes, your cells that produce melanin, to destroy your organ, your skin. I renounce the enemy that wills to harm and hurt you. I curse suspicious-looking moles and unusual growths that are taking root and developing on your skin. I speak death to these growths and command them to die off at their seed and to dry up at their root and to fall off your body in Jesus' name. I release the healing power of the Lord Jesus Christ to flow in and throughout melanocytes to re-create them and restore them so that they can do their job and produce the proper amount of melanin to protect your skin from the harmful rays of the sun. I believe in the power of His mercy and grace toward you to cleanse, to heal, and to make you whole again. In His precious name I pray in faith for you, amen.

Confession of Faith

According to God's Word, greater is Jesus in me than the enemy, the devil, is in this world (1 John 4:4). Jesus gave me all His authority to use against the wicked attacks of the enemy, including melanoma (Luke 10:19). By faith I activate this supernatural authority, and I voice-activate it and speak death to melanoma and suspicious-looking moles and unusual growths taking root and developing on my skin. I command these growths to die off at their seed, dry up at their root, and fall off my body in Jesus' name. I declare by faith in the power of the redemptive blood of the Lamb of God, Jesus Christ, that my melanocytes are strong and healthy; they produce the proper amount of melanin to protect my skin from the harmful rays of the sun. In the name of Jesus, I believe and receive His miraculous power within me, amen.

Part 6

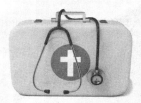

EAR CONDITIONS/DISEASES

Acoustic Neuroma/Noncancerous Tumor

Prayer of Faith

I exercise my authority in Jesus (Luke 10:19) on your behalf against this noncancerous tumor, acoustic neuroma. I curse this tumor and command it to die off at the seed and to dry up at the root and to be supernaturally eliminated from your body. I release the healing power of the Lord to flow through the main vestibular nerve from your inner ear to your brain to cleanse it from all residues of this tumor. I declare by faith that the hearing loss, ringing in the ears, and the unsteady feeling are healed in Jesus' name, amen.

Confession of Faith

In the name of Jesus, I decree by faith that this noncancerous tumor dies off at the seed and dries up at the root and is supernaturally gone for my wellbeing. I trade in this label, acoustic neuroma, for God's label, redeemed from this curse (Gal. 3:13). I claim by faith what is legally mine—healing by the power of the blood of Jesus (Isa. 53:4-5). By the power of life in my words (Prov. 18:21), I speak forth His healing promise. Hearing loss, ringing in the ears, and this unsteady feeling are all healed. Amen.

Acute Otitis Media/Middle Ear Infection

Prayer of Faith

By faith, I release the healing power of the Lord to flow through your middle ear to cleanse it from all infection caused by bacteria or viruses. I renounce reoccurring infections too. I declare by faith that you are delivered from this curse (Gal. 3:13); your middle ear is re-created, realigned, and all scarring is gone too, amen.

Confession of Faith

I confess by faith that my middle ears are healed in Jesus' name. They are delivered from this curse of acute otitis media (middle ear infections). I believe and receive His healing power into my middle ears to cleanse them from infection caused by bacteria or viruses. All pain and scarring are supernaturally gone. My inner ears are realigned and infection-proof, amen.

Auditory Processing Disorder

Prayer of Faith

In the name of the Lord, I believe (Acts 3:16). I renounce this auditory processing disorder that is causing difficulty in your life. I release the healing power of Jesus to flow through your brain to correct this disorder so that you can process sounds correctly. In faith, I pray, amen.

Confession of Faith

I believe and receive the power of the Lord to heal me from auditory processing disorder (1 Pet. 2:24). This same healing virtue flows through the pathway of sounds from my ears to my brain and heals them. I can process sounds correctly in Jesus' name, amen.

Benign Paroxysmal Positional Vertigo (BPPV)

Prayer of Faith

In Jesus' name, I renounce this diagnosis of BPPV. Jesus redeemed you from this curse at Calvary (Gal. 3:13). I release His healing virtue to flow into your inner ear. This problem of tiny calcium crystals (otoconia) becoming loose from their normal location is healed, and the false sensation of spinning or movement stops in Jesus' name, amen.

Confession of Faith

I believe in the power of the blood of Jesus to heal me from this curse of BPPV (Gal. 3:13). I receive His healing power to flow into my inner ear and to heal me from this problem of tiny calcium crystals becoming loose from their normal location. With the authority given to me by my Lord (Luke 10:19), I command this false sensation of spinning and moving to cease in His name, amen.

Cholesteatoma

Prayer of Faith

I stand in faith believing without wavering (James 1:6) with you, that you are healed from this cholesteatoma—this non-cancerous growth that forms behind or from your eardrum. I curse this growth at its seed and command it to dry up at its root and to be supernaturally eliminated from your body. I plead the power of the blood to protect and to restore your hearing. In His mighty name, I pray, amen.

Confession of Faith

I do not doubt but believe in the healing power of the Lord (James 1:6). I align my faith with His healing promise that by His stripes I am healed (Isa. 53:4-5). I am delivered from this curse (Gal. 3:13), and this noncancerous growth, cholesteatoma, has no power over me because He heals this disease attacking my hearing (Ps. 103:2-3). With the power of life and death in my words (Prov. 18:21), I curse this growth at its seed and command it to dry up at its root and to be supernaturally gone in Jesus' name, amen.

Deafness

Prayer of Faith

By the creative power of words (Gen. 1), let's travel down the pathway of hearing together. With words of faith, we speak things into being that are not as if they already were (Rom. 4:17). By faith, the outer ear is supernaturally re-formed, free from deformities, sickness, and unwanted growths and able to catch and carry the sound waves so they can travel through the ear canal. With the same power of faith-filled words, your auditory (ear) canal is free from allergic reactions, skin conditions, blockages, infections and abscesses, narrow passageways, and growths; it funnels the sound waves to your eardrum. Your eardrum is strong and intact and healed from infections, ruptures, scarring, holes, and free from tinnitus and vertigo. All damage to the eardrums be healed and made whole so they can properly vibrate so these sound waves can travel to the middle ear for the glory of the Lord. I speak re-creation into the three small bones of your middle ear, the hammer, anvil, and stirrup. The movement from the middle ear causes pressure waves that make the fluid inside the cochlea move. I judge my God faithful to keep His promise of healing and restoration to your hearing (Heb. 11:11). Your cochlea inside the inner ear is re-created and able to perform its function, and the tiny hairs inside the cochlea bend and move and convert the movement from sound waves into electrical signals. I stand in faith believing with you that the ears of the deaf are unstopped (Isa. 35:5). These electrical signals are sent to the brain through your auditory nerves, and you hear all the beautiful sounds of creation for the glory of God.

Confession of Faith

I judge my Lord faithful to keep His promise of the healing of my ears (Heb. 11:11). I am not moved by negative reports or by human reasoning that revolts against the power of my faith in His name (Acts 3:16). I declare by faith that I am a noteworthy miracle (Acts 4:16). By the power of life in my words (Prov. 18:21), my outer ear is re-created and positioned correctly, free from deformities, sickness, and unwanted growths, and is able to catch and carry sound waves through the ear canal. With the same power of faith in my words, my auditory (ear) canal is free from allergic reactions, skin conditions, blockages, infections and abscesses, narrow passageways, and growths; it funnels the sound waves to my eardrum. My eardrums are strong and healthy and healed from infections, ruptures, scarring, holes, and free from tinnitus and vertigo. All damage to the eardrums be healed and made whole and vibrate properly so these sound waves can travel to my middle ears. I receive the power of re-creation into these three small bones in my middle ears, the hammer, anvil, and stirrup. The movement from my middle ear causes pressure waves that make the fluid inside my cochlea move. My cochlea are re-created and able to perform their function, and the tiny hairs inside the cochlea bend and move and convert the movement from sound waves into electrical signals. I stand in faith believing without wavering (James 1:6) that the ears of the deaf are unstopped (Isa. 35:5), including my ears. These electrical signals are sent to the brain through my auditory nerves, and I can hear loud and soft noises and high and low pitches all for the glory of my Lord, amen.

Eardrum Rupture

Prayer of Faith

In the name of Jesus, I pray in faith over your eardrum. I release the healing power of the Lord to flow in and throughout it. The tear in the thin membrane that separates your outer ear and your inner ear is supernaturally mended, strengthened, and protected from future ruptures and infections. Amen.

Confession of Faith

I decree words of faith over my eardrum. I declare that by His wounds this wound is healed and made whole (1 Pet. 2:24). I command the tear in the thin membrane in my eardrum to be supernaturally healed and strengthened and not to rupture again. By faith, my ears are free from bad bacteria, water, and foreign objects, amen.

Meniere's Disease/Vertigo

Prayer of Faith

In Jesus' name, I pray words of faith over you. I renounce this curse, Meniere's disease (vertigo), affecting your inner ear. I release the healing power of the Lord to flow through your inner ear to cleanse and heal it from viral infections, autoimmune disorders, poor fluid drainage, extra fluid (endolymph), and genetics and to strengthen it from future infections and other attacks, dizzy spells, ringing in the ear, and hearing loss. In the name of Jesus, be healed and hear well. Amen.

Confession of Faith

I believe in the healing power of Jesus (Isa. 53:4-5) and that I am delivered from this curse, Meniere's disease (Gal. 3:13). With the power of life in my words (Prov. 18:21), my inner ears are healed from vertigo, viral infections, autoimmune disorders, poor fluid drainage, extra fluid (endolymph) in my ears, and genetics. I am loosed from this infirmity (Luke 12:13); my ears are free from future infections and healed from a present infection, dizzy spells, ringing in my ears, and hearing loss. By His wounds, I am healed (1 Pet. 2:24). Amen.

Swimmer's Ear

Prayer of Faith

In Jesus' name, I renounce this infection, swimmer's ear. I release the healing power of the blood of Jesus to flow through your outer ear canal and eardrum. I renounce standing, stagnant water in your ear and the growth of bacteria in it. Be healed and pain-free, amen.

Confession of Faith

By the power of life and death in my words (Prov. 18:21), I speak death to the bad bacteria in my outer ear canal and eardrum. I receive His healing power inside my ear and am delivered from this curse (Gal. 3:13) and am protected from any future infections that would try to come upon my ears. In His name, I base my faith for my healing (Acts 3:16). Amen.

Tinnitus

Prayer of Faith

In the name of Jesus your Healer (Exod. 15:26), I renounce this tinnitus tormenting you. I curse this ringing, whistling, clicking, and roaring that you hear. I release the healing power of Jesus to flow through your ears to heal them of these symptoms and the underlying cause of it, amen.

Confession of Faith

I believe in the healing power of the blood of Jesus (Isa. 53:4-5), and I receive His healing virtue inside of my ears. I speak words of faith over myself (Prov. 18:21) and decree that I am delivered from this torment, and I demand in the name of Jesus that all ringing, whistling, clicking, and roaring sounding inside my ears ceases and the underlying cause is healed by the power of His wounds (1 Pet. 2:24). Amen.

Part 7

EYE CONDITIONS/DISEASES

Adie's Tonic Pupil

Prayer of Faith

In the name of Jesus, I stand in faith believing without wavering (James 1:6) against this neurological disorder attacking your eyes. With words of faith (Prov. 18:21), I speak destruction to this eye disease, Adie's tonic pupil, that is harming your eyes. I release the healing salve of Jesus, His redemptive blood to flow through your nervous system—the brain, spinal cord, and nerves. This involuntary function of the pupil will respond appropriately to the light in Jesus' mighty name, amen.

Confession of Faith

In Jesus' name, I am loosed from this infirmity (Luke 13:12). By the power of my faith in His name (Acts 3:16), I am delivered from this curse (Gal. 3:13). With the power of life in my words (Prov. 18:21), my nervous system—my brain, spinal cord, and nerves—is re-created, and my pupils respond correctly to the light in Jesus' name. I put my faith in God's promise that I shall decree a thing, and it shall be established to me: and the light shall shine upon my ways (Job 22:28). Amen.

Amblyopia (Lazy Eye)

Prayer of Faith

In the name of Jesus, I renounce this eye disorder, amblyopia (lazy eye). With the creative power of our words (Gen. 1, Prov. 18:21, Rom. 4:17) I speak to your eye and to your brain, and command that they work together, and both eyes see perfectly well, amen.

Confession of Faith

God's Word says that I have power in my words (Gen. 1; Prov. 18:21; Rom. 4:17) So, I use the power of my words to release the Lord's healing power. In Jesus' name, I am healed from lazy eye. My brain and my eye work together as God created them to do, and both my eyes are strong and healthy, and they see perfectly well. Amen.

Blepharitis/Anterior and Posterior

Prayer of Faith

In the name of Jesus, I renounce the inflammation of your eyelids. I curse this label, blepharitis, and the suffering it is causing you. I release the healing power of the Lord to flow through the oil glands near the base of the eyelashes. I command them to come unclogged and all irritation and redness leave. In Jesus' name I pray, amen.

Confession of Faith

I stand in faith believing without wavering (James 1:6) that my eyelids are healed from blepharitis. I curse all bad bacteria that are harming my eyelids. I speak health and wellness to my meibomian glands and command them to be supernaturally cleansed and delivered from uncontrolled bacterial growth. In the name of Jesus, my eyelids are healed and all irritations, including burning, itching, tearing, redness, and gritty feeling in my eyes, is healed and made whole, fully functional without all the torment. I declare the Word of the Lord over my eyes that they are healed by the power of His healing blood (Isa. 53:4-5). Amen and amen.

Blindness

Prayer of Faith

In the mighty name of Jesus, I renounce this spirit of blindness robbing your vision. As Jesus used dirt and spit to re-create the eyes of the blind man (John 9:6), I use the Word of God and the power of Holy Spirit, and I release the creative and miracle power of the Lord to flow through your optic nerves and all parts of your eyes and the eyeballs themselves. I command them to obey the Word of the Lord, to be re-created, healed, and seeing in Jesus' name, amen.

Confession of Faith

In Jesus' name, I am healed from blindness by the power of the blood that was released through His wounds during Calvary (Isa. 53:4-5). With the power of life in my words (Prov. 18:21), I speak life to dead eyes (Rom. 4:17). I release the same power that raised Jesus Christ from the dead into them (Eph. 1:19-20) My optic nerves and all parts of my eyes and even my eyeballs themselves are re-created, healed, and they see for the glory of the Lord. By faith in His name (Acts 3:16) I see light, I see objects, I see colors, and I can even see details. I stand on His healing promise that the eyes of the blind will be opened (Isa. 35:6)!

Cataracts

Prayer of Faith

I pray in faith without wavering (James 1:6) over your eyes. I renounce these cataracts and vision loss in Jesus' name. Like our God does in Genesis 1, I use the power of faith-filled words and I speak re-creation into the lenses of your eyes. I call things that are not as though they already were (Rom. 4:17) and declare that there is sufficient protein in the lenses of your eyes; they do not clump together to form cataracts. To former cataracts I command the lenses to be refreshed and strengthened (Ps. 41:3), all cloudiness gone, and by faith in the power of the blood Jesus shed to purchase your healing, the lenses of your eyes are re-created, healed, and they can see clearly now. Amen.

Confession of Faith

By the power of my faith in the redemptive blood of Jesus, my eyes are healed from cataracts. I declare words of life and healing into the lenses of my eyes—they are not cloudy but clear. I have sufficient protein in my lenses; these proteins do not clump together and form cataracts. They are refreshed and strengthened (Ps. 41:3), and I can see both far and near. I see light, I see colors, I see objects, and even minute details clearly. I stand on His healing promise that He gives sight to the blind (Luke 4:18)! Amen.

Corneal Conditions

Prayer of Faith

In the name of the Lord our God, I pray in faith without wavering (James 1:6) over the corneas of your eyes. I declare words of faith (Rom. 4:17) that they are loosed from infirmities (Luke 12:13). All abrasions and scarring be made whole; irritations from allergies be healed; inflammation, redness, and swelling be at peace; dry eyes be refreshed; and tear ducts be healed and produce tears. Cloudy vision from buildup of material on the cornea be cleansed and healed in Jesus' name, amen.

Confession of Faith

In Jesus' name, the corneas of my eyes are refreshed and strengthened (Ps. 41:3); they are healed by the wounds that Jesus bore for me at Calvary (1 Pet. 2:24). They are loosed from all infirmities (Luke 12:13). With the power of life in my words (Prov. 18:21), all abrasions and scarring be made whole; irritations from allergies be healed; inflammation, redness, and swelling be at peace; dry eyes be refreshed; and tear ducts be healed and produce tears. Cloudy vision from buildup of material on them be cleansed and healed, amen.

Diabetic Retinopathy

Prayer of Faith

In Jesus' name, I renounce this effect on your eyes and vision from diabetes. I curse both this label and the harm it has caused to your pancreas and this diagnosis of diabetic retinopathy and the harm it has caused to your vision. Yet I believe in the healing power of the Lord Jesus Christ who gives sight to the blind (Luke 4:18), and I obey His command to lay hands on the sick and they will recover (Mark 16:17-18). In Jesus' name, be healed! Amen.

Confession of Faith

I believe in the healing power of the Lord. I receive His promise to restore sight to the blind (Luke 4:18) and to loosen me from this infirmity (Luke 12:13). I declare words of faith over my retinas and command the swelling and leaking fluid to cease in Jesus' name. I decree a stop to the growth of new blood vessels on the surface of my retinas. I renounce a spirit of blindness; this disease, diabetic retinopathy; and the root cause of this issue, diabetes. I declare by faith that my pancreas is re-created, healed, and fully functional in the name of the Lord, my Healer (Exod. 15:26). Amen!

Type 1 Diabetes

See page 70 under "Autoimmune Disorders."

Type 2 Diabetes

See page 229 under "Pancreas Disorders."

Fuchs' Dystrophy

Prayer of Faith

In the name of Jehovah Rapha, the Lord who heals (Exod. 15:26), I renounce this fluid buildup in the cornea of your eye and the swelling and thickening of your cornea. I speak life (Prov. 18:21) into your endothelial cells so that they function as they were created to, doing their job to bring balance of fluid in your cornea and prevent it from swelling. I command the eye discomfort to dissipate and your vision to be clear, not cloudy or blurry, and you can see perfectly without glaring of the vision. In Jesus' name I pray, amen.

Confession of Faith

In the name of the Lord, I am delivered from Fuchs' dystrophy. I am healed from this disease and from the fluid buildup and the swelling and the thickening of my corneas too. My endothelial cells are re-created and function well. These cells do bring balance of the fluid in my corneas and prevent them from swelling. My eyes are free from discomfort; my vision is clear, not cloudy or blurry; and I can see perfectly without glares. In the power of His blood to heal, I pray without wavering (James 1:6) that yes indeed, my corneas, endothelial cells, and vision are healed for the glory of the Lord, amen.

Glaucoma

Prayer of Faith

In the name of Jesus, I renounce this spirit of blindness and eye disease, glaucoma, attacking your optic nerve. I release the healing power of the Great Physician, Jesus, to flow through your optic nerve and trabecular meshwork to re-create them. I command the excessive fluid, aqueous humor, to drain properly, to release you from the pain of eye pressure. I speak creative power into your corneas. Eyes, be delivered from glaucoma and its nasty symptoms. I speak to your vision to be refreshed and strengthened (Ps. 41:3). I declare that you see in Jesus' name, amen and amen.

Confession of Faith

In the name of the Lord my God, I am delivered from this spirit of blindness and eye disease, glaucoma, attacking my optic nerves. I believe without wavering (James 1:6) that I am healed from this disease (Ps. 107:20), all eye pressure is gone, and my eyes and ability to see are refreshed and strengthened (Ps. 41:3). I judge God faithful (Heb. 11:11) to keep His promise that He restores sight to the blind (Luke 4:18). Amen.

Strabismus (Cross-eyed)

Prayer of Faith

In Jesus' name, I pray in faith over this eye condition, strabismus. With the authority of Christ given to me (Luke 10:19), I command the six muscles that control your eye movement to be healed and to work together in harmony so that both of your eyes can point in the same direction at the same time. Amen.

Confession of Faith

I decree and it is established for me (Job 22:27) that my eyes are delivered from this condition, strabismus. They are no longer crossed because they are supernaturally healed. I call things that are not as though they already were (Rom. 4:7). The six muscles that control my eye movement are re-created, healed, and strengthened and work in harmony so that my eyes can point in the same direction at the same time. In Jesus' name, I activate my faith without wavering (James 1:6), amen.

Macular Degeneration

Prayer of Faith

In the name of Jesus, I pray in faith against this eye disease, macular degeneration, which is injuring your macula. I release the creative miracle power of the Lord to flow through the central portion of your retina, specifically the macula, to refresh, strengthen, and to heal it (Ps. 41:3). I declare that your vision is 20/20 for the glory of the Lord, amen.

Confession of Faith

I believe in the promise of the Lord—that He gives sight to the blind (Luke 4:18). With the power of my words (Prov. 18:21), I renounce this degenerative eye disease, macular degeneration. I put my trust in the healing power of the name of Jesus (Acts 3:16). I declare by faith that the central portion of my retina, my macula, is re-created, strengthened, healed (Ps. 41:3). I see perfectly normally for the glory of the Lord and for my wellbeing, amen.

Nystagmus (Dancing Eye)

Prayer of Faith

In the name of Jesus, I renounce this disease, nystagmus affecting, the movement of your eyes. I speak peace to the back part of your brain (brain stem or cerebellum) and healing to your inner ear balance mechanisms. I command your eyes to focus properly, without uncontrolled up and down, side to side, or circular motion. I declare by faith that your brain can control your eye movements. In Jesus' name, amen.

Confession of Faith

By faith in His name (Acts 3:16), I am delivered from this curse, nystagmus, dancing eyes (Gal. 3:13). With the power of faith-filled confessions (Rom. 4:17), the back part of my brain (brain stem or cerebellum) is healed and made whole by the power of His redemptive blood (1 Pet. 2:24). The movement of my eyes no longer has a mind of its own, dancing around uncontrollably from side to side, up and down, or twirling around in circles. No, my brain has control over their movement. In Jesus' name, I pray in faith without wavering, doubt, or unbelief (James 1:6). Amen.

Retinal Detachment

Prayer of Faith

In the name of Jesus, I renounce this spirit of blindness and retinal detachment. I plead the power of the blood over your retina. I command it to move back to its rightful position, the retinal cells and the layer of blood vessels move back together as they should be, so that your eye can receive oxygen and nourishment from these blood vessels. Your vision is supernaturally restored for your wellbeing and for the glory of the Lord, amen.

Confession of Faith

I stand on the healing promise that Jesus restores sight to the blind (Luke 4:18), including me. I declare bold statements of faith (Rom. 4:17): I am delivered from a spirit of blindness and healed from retinal detachment. My retina is back in its rightful position; my retinal cells and the layer of my blood vessels move back together so that my eye can receive oxygen and nourishment from these blood vessels. My vision is supernaturally restored and strengthened (Ps. 41:3), and I can see clearly now. Amen.

Part 8

FEMALE DISORDERS

Breast Cancer

Prayer of Faith

By the power that Jesus released at Calvary, I pray in faith for you that you are delivered from premature death, breast cancer, a possible generational curse, a familiar spirit, and from a spirit of fear. I command in the name of Jesus, all cancerous cells and tumors in your body die off at their seed and dry up at their root and be supernaturally gone from your body, never to return or to spread to other parts of your body. I stand in faith with you that the DNA of the cells in your breasts surrenders to the mighty hand of God's design for it. There is no longer an overproduction of cells that form tumors, but they live and die and complete their healthy, God-created life cycle. I make a bold statement of faith that you are healed from this attack and free from all pain and suffering, and your breasts are re-created. In the mighty name of Jesus, amen.

Confession of Faith

I believe in the healing power of my Savior, Jesus Christ, and that He is faithful and true, willing, and able to heal me (Luke 5:12-13) from a spirit of premature death, breast cancer, cancerous cells, and tumors. I decree an impenetrable wall of protection around every cell, tissue, organ, and system of my body from this cancerous attack. I will be strong and courageous, not afraid or discouraged (Josh. 1:9), for You have not given me a spirit of fear but of power, of love, and of a sound mind (2 Tim. 1:7). With all the authority of Christ given to me over the devil's wicked works (Luke 10:19), I command all cancerous cells and tumors to die off at their seed and to dry up at their root and to be supernaturally eliminated from my milk-producing ducts, my glandular tissue (lobules), and in all other cells and tissues of my breasts, my lymph nodes, and other parts of my body. I demand that the DNA in the cells of my breasts surrenders to the mighty hand of the Lord's design for it. They stop this abnormal overproduction of cells that form into tumors; the cells live and die as they complete their normal, healthy life cycle. I declare words of faith that the DNA in my breast cells is transformed from abnormal to normal. I am delivered and healed from breast cancer, and their shape, size, and functionality are re-created. My every cell, tissue, organ, and system of my body is cancer-free and remains forever free, cancer-proof, and all pain and suffering stops in Jesus' mighty name, amen and amen.

Cervical Cancer

Prayer of Faith

In the name of Jehovah Rapha, your Healer, I renounce this spirit of death, this diagnosis of cervical cancer, HPV (human papillomavirus), cancerous cells, and tumors. I release His power of mercy and grace over you to cleanse the cells of your cervix from cancer. I speak words of faith over your cell's DNA to be re-created, abnormal and cancerous cells to die off and be eliminated from your body, and new healthy cells to be produced. They fulfill God's original design: they live and they die and complete their normal life cycle; therefore, they cannot overpopulate and form tumors. I declare that they support your life and do not destroy it. Your cervix is re-created and you are free from all pain and suffering.

If this disease developed as a result on an ungodly and unhealthy lifestyle, then I pray that you will ask God for forgiveness, accept His forgiveness, move forward and follow God's ways, and experience the deep love that He has for you. In His mighty name I pray in faith for you, amen.

Confession of Faith

I call upon the name of the Lord and for His mercy and grace to manifest in my body. I renounce a spirit of death and this diagnosis of cervical cancer, HPV, cancerous cells, and tumors. I command my cells in my cervix to healed and re-created and to function according to God's great design—they live and die and complete their normal life cycle. They cannot over-produce and form tumors anymore. I command all abnormal and cancerous cells to be supernaturally eliminated from my body. I receive the power of the blood that was shed at Calvary for my healing, and I declare that I will not die but live and declare the works of the Lord (Ps. 118:17). He is my Lord who heals me (Exod. 15:26). In His precious name, I humbly confess His willingness to heal me from this disease and all the pain and suffering that it causes (Luke 5:12-13). I stand in faith believing for the re-creation of my cervix, amen.

Dysmenorrhea (Menstrual Cramps)

Prayer of Faith

By the power of the blood that flowed at Calvary, I pray in faith for you during this time of suffering from severe menstrual cramps. With the power of the spoken word (Rom. 4:17), I speak words of faith into your female organs. In Jesus' name, I say to the uterus to be at peace and strong contractions settle down in the name of the Lord, amen.

Confession of Faith

Lord Jesus, I call upon Your healing virtue to flow through my female organs (Luke 8: 46). I declare by faith in Your all-powerful name that these strong contractions inside my uterus settle down and be at peace. In Your name, I decree this so (Job 22:28), amen.

Endometrial Cancer

Prayer of Faith

In the name Jehovah Rapha, the God who heals you (Exod. 15:26), I pray for you in faith and believe that you are delivered from this spirit of death, this diagnosis of endometrial cancer, cancerous cells, and tumors attacking your uterus. I believe without wavering in the faith for creative miracles to manifest throughout your uterus. The layer of cells that form the lining of your uterus and the DNA of these cells are re-created, and they function to perfection according to God's original design. They do not overpopulate and form tumors, nor can they spread to other parts of your body. They support your life and not steal your life. I declare that you will not die but live and declare the works of the Lord (Ps. 118:17). All pain and suffering stops. In Jesus' name, I pray this over you, amen.

Confession of Faith

By my faith in the healing power of the blood of Jesus (Isa. 53:4-5), I renounce this spirit of death, endometrial cancer, cancerous cells, and tumors attacking my uterus. I receive the His healing touch (Luke 8:45) in my endometrium. This layer of cells that form the lining of my uterus and the DNA of these cells are re-created, strong, and healthy. They are transformed from abnormal to normal; they are no longer out of control but under the control and boundary of God's original design. They grow and multiply at a set rate and die off at a set time. I take a bold stance of faith, and I do not allow abnormal cells to accumulate and form tumors. I decree a wall of protection between cancerous cells and nearby tissues, and they will not metastasize to other parts of my body. I take another bold step of faith and command all cancerous and abnormal cells and tumors to die off and to be gone supernaturally! I am at peace because my faith in my Healer, Jesus Christ, has made me well (Luke 8:48) and has delivered me from all pain and suffering. I stand in faith for my entire reproductive system to be re-created and made whole, amen.

Endometriosis

Prayer of Faith

In the name of your Healer, Jehovah Rapha, I renounce the confusion taking place within your female organs. I curse the endometrial tissue growing outside of your uterus that is trying to attach itself to your ovaries and fallopian tubes, and I command it to get back into the uterus where it belongs. I take my authority in Christ over this abnormal bleeding, severe cramps, and pain before and during your period. In the name of the Lord, I pray, amen.

Confession of Faith

In the name of the Lord my God, I stand firm believing in the healing power of Jehovah Rapha that my female organs are healed and are in proper working order. I do not accept endometriosis. I command the destructive spirit behind this disease to get out of my body and leave my uterus, ovaries, and fallopian tubes alone. I demand the endometrial tissue to get back into my uterus where it belongs, the excessive bleeding to cease, and the severe cramping and pain to settle down before and during my period. I claim my legal right to this healing for the glory of my Lord, amen.

Fibroids (All Types)

Prayer of Faith

I lift a prayer of faith up to Father God on your behalf against these fibroids growing in your body. I curse them at their very seed and command them to dry up at their root, to die off, and to be supernaturally eliminated from your body, never to come back to life or produce again. With all the authority of Christ given to His followers, I charge the heavy bleeding and the blood clots they cause to stop altogether, and the weakness and anemia they produce to be healed. I declare by faith that you are healed, delivered from this bloody curse, and loosed from this infirmity and the shame it carries. For the glory of the Lord, amen and amen.

Confession of Faith

I confess words of faith over my body in the name of the Lord my God, who has delivered me from this bloody curse by becoming the supreme sacrifice and who shed His blood for me so I do not have to bleed day and night. I curse all fibroids in my body. I do not give them permission to live, grow, or to remain in or on my uterus. The heavy bleeding, blood clots, weakness, and anemia they produce must stop and depart from me. With all the authority of my Redeemer, Jesus Christ, I curse every fibroid no matter how big or small they may be at their very seed and root, and they shall not remain in my body. I shout words of victory, "I am redeemed from them, and they have no power over me." In the mighty name of the One, Jesus, who has loosed me from all shame and this infirmity, I rejoice that I am healed! Amen.

Incontinence

Prayer of Faith

In the name of your Messiah and Healer, Yeshua, I pray in faith, believing with you that you are delivered from this weakness and the shame of a leaky bladder. I speak to your bladder and to the muscles, ligaments, tendons, nerves, and nerve endings surrounding it to be supernaturally strengthened for your good and for the ability to control your bladder functions, in the name of the Lord Most High, amen.

Confession of Faith

In the name of the Lord, I confess every day that my bladder and the muscles, ligaments, tendons, nerves, and nerve endings that surround it are no longer weak but strong by the healing power of my Lord. Your Word says in Luke 1:45

(NIV), *"Blessed is she who has believed that the Lord would fulfill His promises to her."* I believe this to be true, and by the power of my faith in the finished work of Christ I am healed from a leaky bladder, amen.

Infertility

Prayer of Faith

In the name of Jesus, I renounce the spirit of death and this label of Infertility and the power of barrenness behind it. I release the healing power of the blood of Jesus to flow through your hormones and reproductive organs to re-create, to heal, and to give them strength to conceive. I plead the power of the blood of Christ to protect your eggs as they make that journey to meet the seed of their father inside your fallopian tube. As this little one is conceived, they are firmly planted within your uterus and grow safely within your womb. I pray strength to your body to carry your baby to full term and that you give birth to a strong, healthy, and happy baby so that your joy will be fulfilled as you raise your child for the glory of the Lord, amen and amen.

Confession of Faith

I am blessed because I believe the Lord will fulfill His promise to me (Luke 1:45). Give to me the desire of my heart (Rom. 12:2)—a strong, healthy, and happy baby. I stand firm in my faith that by His stripes (Isa. 53:5) my hormones and reproductive organs are healed, strengthened, and made whole. My hope has transformed into faith, and I believe soon I will hold my child and nurture them for the glory of the Lord, amen.

Menopause

Prayer of Faith

I pray for you, dear sister, as you pass through this change in your life, that your mind and emotions will stay intact as you keep your spiritual eyes fixed on the Lord. He is faithful and true; He will never leave you nor forsake you. You can trust Him to give you the grace to walk forward with all joy. I pray that though this change is great, the symptoms for you will be mild. Remember when you feel weak in Him you can remain strong. He is your strength and all that you need. In Jesus' name I pray, amen.

Confession of Faith

I confess by faith the goodness and the mercy of God upon me that I pass through this change in my life with grace. I will not fear this time in my life, for God has not given me a spirit of fear but of power, of love, and of a sound mind (2 Tim. 1:7). I know that I have been redeemed from the power of the curse (Gal. 3:13) and trust in my God to keep His promises to me (Luke 1:45), not to give me more than I can handle (1 Cor. 10:13). His joy is my strength (Neh. 8:10), and I take my daily dose of laughter as it does me good like medicine (Prov. 17:22). I keep the promises of God in the center of my heart, for they are life and health to my body (Prov. 4:20-22). I will not accept the negative words that the world has to say about this change in my life, but I will listen only to pleasant words for they are sweet to my mind and healing to my body (Prov. 16:24). This I will confess daily over my life, amen.

Miscarriage (Threatened or Repeated)

Prayer of Faith

In the name of Jesus, I renounce this spirit of death over the baby in your womb. By faith, I command your cervix to remain closed for the duration of this full-term pregnancy and this bleeding and pelvic cramping to stop. I plead His healing power over the health and wellbeing of the baby and that your baby develops into a strong and healthy child with no physical issues or intellectual challenges. I believe in a compassionate God, and with Him all things are possible. In Jesus' name, I pray in faith, amen.

Confession of Faith against Threatened Miscarriage

Lord, like Sarah, I judge You faithful (Heb. 11:11). No matter how negative the medical report may be, I choose to believe in Your report (Isa. 53:1) that declares by Your wounds baby and I are healed and made whole (Isa. 53:4-5). I know that with You all things are possible (Mark 10:27). With Your authority given to me (Luke 10:19), I command my cervix to remain closed for the duration of this full-term pregnancy and this bleeding and pelvic cramping to stop in Jesus' name. I plead the healing power of the blood of Jesus over the health and wellbeing of my child within my womb and that this precious little one will develop into a strong, healthy, and happy baby with no physical issues or intellectual challenges. In Jesus' name, amen.

Confession of Faith against Recurrent Miscarriage

In the name of Jehovah Rapha, the God who heals (Exod. 15:26), I stand on the promise of Your Word, and by Your stripes my female organs are healed (Isa. 53:4-5). I take a bold

Confession of Faith

I do not doubt in the power of my Lord to heal me as I boldly renounce a spirit of fear and the spirit of death, any familiar spirit from a possible generational curse, ovarian cancer, all cancerous cells, and tumors attacking my body. I renounce this abnormal growth of cells (tumors) that has formed in or near my ovaries. I command them to die off at their seed and dry up at the root and to be supernaturally eliminated from my body. I demand that these cells stop over-multiplying and forming tumors, and they cease invading and destroying my healthy body tissue. I command my DNA in these cells to surrender to the Word of the Lord that declares by His stripes I am healed (Isa. 53:4-5). By the power of my faith in the redemptive blood of Jesus, I shout, "Yes, and amen!" for the normal production of healthy cells that are cancer-free and cancer-proof all the days of my life. All damage that has occurred from medical procedures is healed by faith. I am delivered from all pain and suffering. I stand in faith, believing that my ovaries and my entire reproductive system is re-created, in Jesus' name, amen.

Polycystic Ovary Syndrome (PCOS)

Prayer of Faith

I pray in faith over your reproductive organs and your hormones that they are delivered from a spirit of death and PCOS. I stand in faith with you for a creative miracle to take place within your ovaries, follicles, and eggs. All is re-created, in their rightful positions, and fulfilling their daily and monthly functions with God's precision. With the re-creation of your ovaries, your menstrual cycle begins to cycle in a normal fashion, not too long and not too short. I command the cysts on the outer edge of the ovaries to be gone and not to return. The high levels of the hormone androgen to begin to lower to a balanced level, and the excessive facial and body hair, severe acne, and male-pattern baldness stop. I decree a wall of protection between you and type 2 diabetes and heart disease. In Jesus' name, I pray in faith believing, amen.

Confession of Faith

In the name of my Creator, Jesus Christ, I confess over my reproductive organs daily the healing power of His Word—that by His stripes I am healed from a spirit of death and PCOS. I declare the healing promise that He has redeemed me from this curse and that the desire of my heart to be a mother one day will be fulfilled. I speak words of faith over my ovaries, follicles, and eggs that yes, they are re-created, in their rightful positions, fulfilling their daily and monthly functions with God's precise design for them. My menstrual cycles are normal, not too long and not too short, just right. I do not accept cysts on the outer edge of my ovaries. I hereby give them an eviction notice in the name of the Lord; I command them, "Get out!" in Jesus' name. I speak balance to my hormone levels, especially to the hormone androgen, to obey my voice and to lower to a balanced level. I speak to the production of excessive facial and body hair, severe acne, and male-pattern baldness to stop. I decree a wall of protection between me and type 2 diabetes and heart disease. You will not have me, spirit of death, for I am filled with the life of God in me. In Jesus' name, I believe, amen.

Primary Ovarian Insufficiency

Prayer of Faith

In the name of our precious Lord, I pray this prayer of faith for you against this spirit of premature death in your womb. I release the spirit of life—the power of Holy Spirit to resurrect your ovaries. They continue to produce the correct amounts of estrogen and release eggs regularly. I renounce this diagnosis of infertility and declare healthy, strong, and happy babies being raised for the glory of the Lord to be produced and carried to full term in your womb. Our Father God instructs you to call things that do not exist as though they already did, and so I join my faith with your faith for a beautiful family to come forth from your body. Like Sarah does in Hebrews 11:11, I judge my God faithful over you and your desire to be a mom. In His most holy name, I pray, amen.

Confession of Faith

In the name of my Great Physician, Yeshua, I daily confess over my ovaries that they will not die off prematurely but live to produce healthy amounts of estrogen and release healthy eggs regularly. I do not accept this label of primary ovarian insufficiency or the negative power of infertility behind it. Like Sarah from the Bible, I judge my God faithful to keep His promise to me, and I look forward to carrying the fulfillment of His promise to me within my womb and one day in my arms. Children are part of my inheritance, and I will not allow the enemy to steal my children from me. I believe in the God of the impossible, knowing that with Him all things, including this miracle, are possible because I forever judge Him faithful to me, amen.

Toxic Shock Syndrome (TSS)

Prayer of Faith

In the name of the Lord, I renounce this spirit of death and toxic shock syndrome and command it to leave your body in Jesus' name. I renounce these poison-producing strains of bacteria in your bloodstream. I release the healing power of the Lord to flow throughout your streams of blood to purify them of all toxins, and they, along with all of your organs, are cleansed and healed from TSS. In faith I stand without wavering on your behalf (James 1:6). Amen.

Confession of Faith

In the name of Jesus, my Healer, I decree a separation between me and this spirit of death and TSS. I declare that my bloodstream and organs are cleansed and purified by the redemptive power of the blood You shed for me at Calvary, amen.

Turner Syndrome

Prayer of Faith

In the mighty name of Jesus and by the power of His redemptive blood, I pray in faith over you, dear sister, and this attack of the devil against you and one of your X chromosomes with this condition called Turner syndrome. I call upon the creative power of Holy Spirit to re-create this X chromosome that the devil stole from you. I speak to your growth plates to open so that you can grow to a normal height, that your breasts develop, and that you begin to have menstrual cycles with ovaries that are fully developed and begin to produce one egg each month for possible fertilization and to produce the female hormones estrogen and progesterone.

While I pray in faith for you, your heart and kidneys come to my attention. I declare words of faith over your heart: that it is re-created by the same power that raised Jesus from the dead. It works as God designed the heart to function, with no infirmity, no heart murmur, and certainly no weak or missing parts. I speak over those kidneys of yours to be cleansed, re-created, and healed so that they can function according to God's perfect design.

I speak to those possible extras that have been packed in the devil's bag of dirty tricks trying to abide in your body, like the extra skin on the neck. I command this extra skin to shrink away, the lymphedema of the hands and feet to be gone supernaturally, and to any skeletal abnormalities to straighten out with no deficiencies. With God all things are possible, and nothing is too difficult for our Lord, including the re-creation of your body and functions. For the glory of God to be revealed in your life, I pray believing for you, amen.

Confession of Faith

I confess throughout the day and every day that I believe in the God of the impossible and that nothing is too difficult for my God, including the re-creation of my body (Luke 1:37). I am blessed because I believe in Your faithfulness to me (Luke 1:45). By Your stripes I am healed in spirit, soul, and in physical body (Isa. 53:4-5). My faith is the only evidence that I need to know that I am healed (Heb. 11:1). My strength to believe in Your healing promises comes from hearing Your Word (Rom. 10:17).

I take a bold stand of faith that I am delivered and healed from Turner syndrome and all the evil power behind it. I command with words of faith in the most holy name of Jesus that the missing X chromosome supernaturally exists in my body, and it is a good thing. I declare without exception my growth plates reopen, and I grow by the grace of God to a normal height; my breasts develop, I begin to have menstrual cycles with fully developed ovaries, and they begin to produce one egg per month for possible fertilization and the female hormones estrogen and progesterone for the good of my wellbeing.

I make no exceptions for lack in my God-given female body. I speak by the power of the spoken law (Gen. 1) the re-creation of a fully functional heart with no infirmities, no heart murmur, and no weak or missing parts. My kidneys are cleansed, re-created, fully functional, and they do as my Creator God designed them to do.

And to the excessive skin around my neck, I command you gone in Jesus' name. I give an eviction notice to the lymphedema in my hands and feet, the cause of the retention of this excessive fluid be done away with, and for the glory of the Lord my skeletal system is re-created and has no abnormalities and no more pain and suffering. For I truly do believe in the goodness of my God to heal and make me whole. I praise Him, for I am fearfully and wonderfully made (Ps. 139). Amen.

Urinary Tract Infection (UTI)

Prayer of Faith

I stand in faith, believing with you that this infection in your urinary tract be gone by the redemptive power of the blood of Jesus that washes and heals you of all bad bacteria, fungi, or viruses. Your kidneys, ureters, bladder, and urethra are all strong and healthy and function at full capacity as they should, amen.

Confession of Faith

I confess words of faith over my urinary tract that it is no longer plagued by infections, but that my kidneys, ureters, bladder and urethra are strong and healthy and function perfectly normally as God has designed them to filter and allow my urine to pass through in a healthy manner. In the name of Jesus, I confess this to be the case in my body, amen.

Part 9

FUNGAL INFECTIONS

Athlete's Foot/Tinea Pedis

Prayer of Faith

In the name of Jesus your Healer, I renounce the tinea fungus that has grown on your feet. With the power of the spoken word, I speak death to it. I release the healing power of the Lord to flow through your feet to cleanse them from this fungus, and I command the itching and burning to cease. In Jesus' name, be healed, amen.

Confession of Faith

In Jesus' name, I decree a legal order against this tinea fungus. I command it to die off, never to return or to spread again. I speak peace into my feet, and by His stripes my feet are healed and made whole (Isa. 53:5). In Jesus' name, amen.

Nail Fungus/Onychomycosis

Prayer of Faith

In the name of the Lord Jesus Christ, I renounce this nail fungus that plagues you. I declare the Word of the Lord that He was plagued by God at Calvary so you could be free from this plague, nail fungus (Isa. 53:4). Be healed and made whole (Isa. 53:5), amen!

Confession of Faith

Jehovah Rapha, my great physician (Exod. 15:26), Your medical report declares that by Your wounds I am healed from this nail fungus (Isa. 53:4-5). I have been redeemed from this curse, onychomycosis (Gal. 3:13). I put my trust in Your promise to restore health to me and to heal my wounds (Jer. 30:17). I release the creative power of words (Gen. 1) and speak words of life (Prov. 18:21) into my nails. I call things that are not as though they already were (Rom. 4:17). There is no fungus or infection in my nails, my nails are not discolored or thickened, and they do not crumble at the edge. They are strong and healthy as a testimony of Your faithfulness (1 Thess. 5:24). Amen.

Ringworm/Tinea Corporis

Prayer of Faith

In Jesus' name, I renounce this fungal infection, ringworm. I release the healing power of Jesus to flow into the infected area to cleanse and heal it. I speak to the rash to stop itching and to disappear and not to spread or to return. In Jesus' name, I pray in faith, amen.

Confession of Faith

Jesus, I believe that by Your wounds I am healed (1 Pet. 2:24) and I am loosed from this infirmity (Luke 12:13). You bore this fungal infection, ringworm (Matt. 8:17). You delivered me from this itchy curse by becoming the curse for me (Gal. 3:13). I speak words of faith, and this fungal infection is healed; the infected area is made whole for my wellbeing and for the glory of the Lord, amen.

Part 10

GENETIC CONDITIONS AND DISORDERS

Down Syndrome/Trisomy 21

Prayer of Faith

I call upon the mercy of the Miracle Worker, Jesus Christ, on your behalf. I stand in faith believing without wavering (James 1:6) for this undeniable, noteworthy miracle (Acts 4:16) that will take place in your life. With the power of life and death in the tongue (Prov. 18:21), I speak elimination to the third copy or partial copy of your 21st chromosome. Your 21st chromosome is strengthened based on faith in the name of Jesus (Acts 3:16) and restored to God's original design. All physical and mental developmental delays and disabilities are transformed from abnormal to normal, and your life expectancy is extended to a normal lifespan, in Jesus' name, I pray in faith. Amen.

Confession of Faith

By my faith in Jesus' name, my 21st chromosome is healed (Acts 4:16). With the power of my words (Rom. 4:17), I declare that there is no extra copy of this chromosome. I can do all things through Christ who strengthens me (Phil. 4:13). Amen.

Fragile X Syndrome

Prayer of Faith

In the mighty name of Jesus, I pray in faith for you against this debilitating syndrome, Fragile X. Without wavering (James 1:6), I believe that the abnormal breakage of your X chromosome is healed and made whole (Isa. 53:4-5). You are loosed from this infirmity (Luke 12-13) and from all developmental delay and intellectual disability for the glory of God. Amen.

Confession of Faith

In Jesus' name, I am healed.

Muscular Dystrophy

Prayer of Faith

In the name of Jesus, I renounce these spirits of death and infirmity. By the power of death in the tongue (Prov. 18:21), I speak death to these diseases, these abnormal genetic mutations, and all forms of muscular dystrophy. With the same power of our words, I declare things that are not as though they already were (Rom. 4:17). I believe in the power of the blood of Jesus to sustain your life, to refresh your muscular system and the muscles' daily production of proteins, and to strengthen all weaknesses in your body. For the glory of the Lord, your calf muscles are normal sized; you can walk and run, not waddle, and swallow without trouble. I believe in the power of re-creation, and I speak to the heart and lungs to be re-created and to function perfectly normally. I command scoliosis to be gone and your spine be realigned, stiff or loose joints to be healed, and your brain be re-created and to function as it should. In Jesus' name, I pray in faith, amen.

Confession of Faith

In Jesus' name, I am healed. I can breathe, swallow, walk, and talk for God's glory, amen.

Part 11

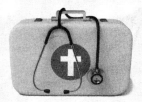

HEART DISEASE

Atrial Fibrillation

Prayer of Faith

With all boldness, I proclaim that you are healed from atrial fibrillation. Your heart is re-created; the upper chambers of your heart are in sync with the lower chambers; it beats beautifully with no irregularities, no palpitations, and no shortness of breath, for you possess the healing power of Christ (Isa. 53:4-5) and Holy Spirit is the very breath that you breathe (Job 33:4), amen.

Confession of Faith

Jehovah-Elohim, the Creator of this world and humanity (Gen. 1:26-28), I enter Your gates with thanksgiving and into Your courts with praise: I am thankful to You, and I bless Your name (Ps. 100:4). I believe and receive the healing power of Your blood into my physical heart (Isa. 53:4-5) and I know that I am loosed from this infirmity, atrial fibrillation (Luke 12:13). I align my faith with all Your authority that You have so graciously gifted to me (Luke 10:19), and by my faith in Your ability and willingness to heal the sick (Luke 5:12-13) I am healed (Ps. 30:2). My heart submits to its Creator and accepts this re-creative miracle, and my upper chambers are in sync with my lower chambers. Atrial fibrillation does not control the workings of my heart, and there is no shortness of breath in me for I possess the breath of Holy Spirit (Job 33:4), and He's got rhythm and knows how to keep the beat. By the creative power of the tongue (Prov. 18:21), I declare that the rhythm of my heart is strong and steady and beats at a regular pace, with no palpitations. This is my testimony (Rev. 12:11): I am healed in Jesus' name, amen.

Atrial Septal Defect

Prayer of Faith

I lift you up to El-Shaddai, Almighty God who has the ability to heal you of this congenital heart defect, atrial septal defect (Rom. 4:21). I praise Him for His willingness to loose you from this infirmity (Luke 12:13) and to create in you a clean heart (Ps. 51:10-12) without defects. With His supernatural power, He sutures the hole between the upper chambers of your heart. By the power of the blood that flows through the holes in His hands, we believe and receive the blessing of healing for you. In the name of Almighty God, El-Shaddai, I pray in faith, amen.

Confession of Faith

I believe in Almighty God, El-Shaddai, and in Your ability to handle any situation that confronts Your people. With confidence in Your ability and willingness to heal me (Luke 5:12-13), I receive the dunamis explosive power of Holy Spirit into the need of my physical heart. Because I ask in faith without wavering back and forth with unbelief (James 1:6), I am loosed from this congenital heart defect, atrial septal defect (Luke 12:13). You have already healed me from this infirmity and the spirit of premature death behind it (Ps. 107:20; Is. 53:4-5). The Great Physician has supernaturally sutured the hole between the upper chambers of my heart, and no excessive amount of blood can flow through my lungs, for I am delivered and healed from atrial septal defect. In the name of Jesus, this is my confession of faith for my heart, health, and wellbeing, amen.

Blood Pressure (High and Low)
High Blood Pressure/Hypertension

Prayer of Faith

Jehovah Rapha, I hold up the shield of faith. I voice-activate the sword of the Spirit (Eph. 6) on your behalf for healing from high blood pressure. I believe in His ability (Rom. 4:21) and in His willingness (Matt. 8:3) to heal you from this illness. I stand in faith that your blood pressure reads 120/80 for the glory of the Lord, amen.

Confession of Faith

I believe in Jehovah Rapha, the Lord who heals my body (Exod. 15:26). I boldly come before Your throne of grace that I may obtain mercy and find grace to help in my time of need (Heb. 4:16). My faith in You makes me well (Luke 8:48), and You remove this sickness of high blood pressure from my midst (Exod. 23:25). You give me wisdom (James 1:5) to change the things in life that I need to change. You heal me from other illnesses (Ps. 103:2-3) that may be causing my blood pressure to rise to dangerous levels. I stand in faith that my blood pressure reads 120/80. I am thankful that You give me Your peace (John 14:27), Your comfort (2 Cor. 1:3-4), and that Your joy is my strength (Neh. 8:10). By your stripes I am healed and made whole (Isa. 53:4-5), amen.

Low Blood Pressure/Hypotension

Prayer of Faith

I raise up the standard of the blood (Isa. 59:19), and by faith I declare that you are delivered from a spirit of premature death and healed from hypotension (Deut. 7:15). I call those things that are not as though they already were (Rom. 4:17), and with these words of faith I declare that your blood pressure rises to 120/80 and remains in the normal range. I claim His healing promise that He satisfy you with long life (Ps. 91:6). This I believe without wavering with doubt and unbelief (James 1:6). In Jesus' name, amen.

Confession of Faith

In the name of the Messiah, Jesus of Nazareth, who delivered me from this curse, hypotension, by becoming the curse for me (Gal. 3:13), I trust in the power of Your blood that purchased my healing (Isa. 53:4-5). By the power of Your blood I am loosed from the bondage of this infirmity of low blood pressure (Luke 12:13). You take away all sickness from me (Deut. 7:15). You satisfy me with long life (Ps. 91:6) and Your joy is my strength and stronghold (Neh. 8:10). I raise up my shield of faith and activate the sword of the Spirit (Eph. 6), and I declare words of life (Prov. 18:21) that my blood pressure raises to 120/80 in Jesus' name, amen and amen.

Cholesterol (High)

Prayer of Faith

In the name of Jesus, I renounce this spirit of premature death attacking your heart. I release the healing power of His blood to flow through your heart to cleanse, heal, and make it whole again so that it functions to perfection. The excess cholesterol and other deposits on the walls of your arteries and fatty deposits in your blood vessels dissolve and are supernaturally eliminated from your system so that enough blood can flow through your arteries. In Jesus' name I pray, amen.

Confession of Faith

With the power of the spoken Word (Gen. 1), I activate the power of life and death in my tongue (Prov. 18:21) and I decree a wall of protection between the effects of high cholesterol and my health and wellbeing. I release the healing power of the Lord (Ps. 30:2) to heal and make my heart whole again. I renounce the excess cholesterol and other deposits on the walls of my arteries and fatty deposits in my blood vessels and command them in the name of Jesus to dissolve and to be supernaturally cleansed from my system so that enough blood can flow through my arteries. In Jesus' name I declare by faith I am healed (Isa. 53:4-5). Amen.

Coronary Artery/Heart Disease

Prayer of Faith

By the grace of God (Rom. 4:16), I stand in faith without wavering with doubt and unbelief (James 1:6) for your deliverance from coronary artery/heart disease. By the redemptive power of the blood of Jesus, you are healed because He has loosed you from this infirmity (Luke 12:13), the curse, when He suffered and died on the Cross (Gal. 3:13). By faith in His healing power, the walls of your arteries are supernaturally cleansed from plaque buildup, restrictions of the blood flow to the heart's muscle are removed, and the coronary arteries are re-created in Jesus' name, amen.

Confession of Faith

I give You praise for You are faithful (1 Thess. 5:24) and just (Deut. 32:4) and both willing (Matt. 8:3) and able (Rom. 4:21) to heal me from this coronary artery/heart disease (Ps. 103:2-3). By the power of faith-filled words (Gen. 1), I declare that this buildup of plaque in the walls of my arteries super-naturally melts away and is eliminated from my body with no residue of this plaque remaining. By the law of grace (Rom. 4:16), the past limitations of the blood flow to my heart's muscle are removed, and I am loosed from the bondage of this infirmity (Luke 12:13) with the re-creation of my coronary arteries intact. Amen.

Heart Attack

Prayer of Faith

All-powerful Jesus, I stand in faith without wavering (James 1:6) knowing that nothing is impossible with You (Mark 10:27). I declare words of faith, that no weapon formed against you will prosper (Isa. 54:17). He heals all diseases, including acute myocardial infarction (heart attacks) (Ps. 103:2-3). By His stripes your heart is healed (Isa. 53:4-5) and re-created, made whole and fully functional, amen and amen.

Confession of Faith

I am not afraid or discouraged but strong and courageous because I know that You are with me wherever I go (Josh. 1:9). I call upon Jehovah-Shalom, my God who defeats this enemy, the spirit of death, and this life-threatening condition, acute myocardial infarction (heart attacks). I receive Your peace into my mind and emotions against this spirit of fear and into the inner workings of my physical heart. Jesus Almighty, all-powerful Lord, nothing is impossible with You (Mark 10:27), including the re-creation of my heart and all damage that has been done to my heart's tissue. I declare words of faith that I will not die but live and declare the works of the Lord (Ps. 118:17). Amen.

Heart Failure/Congestive Heart Failure

Prayer of Faith

I pray in faith, believing not wavering (James 1:6) that you are delivered from this spirit of death and healed (Ps. 103:2-3) from congestive heart failure. I declare that your heart is re-created, and the heart's ventricles are not stretched out but strong and healthy, and it pumps enough blood throughout your entire body. In Jesus' name, amen.

Confession of Faith

I give glory to the God of Hope, Jesus Christ, my Deliverer from this spirit of death, heart failure. You have loosed me from this infirmity (Luke 12:13), redeemed me from this curse (Gal. 3:13), set me free (John 8:36), and by the stripes that wounded You I am healed and made whole (Isa. 53:4-5). By Your Spirit (Zech. 4:6) You give me the victory (1 Cor. 15:57) to stand against the wiles of the devil (Eph. 6:11). I overcome

illness, small vessel disease. I receive the healing power of the blood of Jesus (Isa. 53:4-5). He sustains my life, refreshes the oxygen-rich blood that flows to my heart, and strengthens the walls of my small arteries in my heart (Ps. 41:3). In Jesus' name, amen.

Sudden Cardiac Arrest

Prayer of Faith

In the name of Jesus your Healer, with all the authority He gave to His followers over satan and his wicked works (Luke 10:19), I renounce this spirit of death attacking you with sudden cardiac arrest. I declare with the power of life and death in the tongue (Prov. 18:21) that you will not die but live and declare the works of the Lord (Ps. 118:17). I release the same healing power that raised Jesus from the dead into your body (Rom. 8:11). This supernatural electrical charge empowers your heart. The heart is raised up from this deadly attack and begins to beat with a regular and healthy rhythm; the power of Holy Spirit breathes the breath of life into you (Job 33:4). In Jesus' name, be healed! Amen.

Confession of Faith

I declare that no weapon formed against me shall prosper (Isa. 54:17). I will not die but live and declare the works of the Lord (Ps. 118:17). My heart is re-created and begins to beat with a regular and healthy rhythm. The power of Holy Spirit breathes the breath of life into me, amen.

Ventricular Tachycardia

Prayer of Faith

I lift you up to Abba Father for deliverance from this spirit of death, ventricular tachycardia. With the supernatural power of words of faith (Rom. 4:17), I declare that the electrical signals in the ventricles of your heart are reestablished, free from arrhythmia. The rhythm of your heart beats to perfection for the glory of the Lord and regains its ability to pump enough blood to the rest of the body. Amen.

Confession of Faith

With all the authority of Christ gifted to me (Luke 10:19), I renounce this spirit of death, ventricular tachycardia. I receive His supernatural power into my heart. The electrical signals in the ventricles of my heart are reestablished, free from arrhythmia. The rhythm of my heart beats perfectly and regains its ability to pump enough blood to the rest of my body. For the glory of the Lord, I believe and receive my healing, amen.

Part 12

LIVER DISEASES

Ascites

Prayer of Faith

In the name of Jesus, I lift you up in faith without wavering (James 1:6). You are delivered from these spirits of death and infirmity. I stand in faith that your liver is supernaturally healed from this condition, ascites. Even though the report says this is incurable, I judge Him faithful (Heb. 11:11) to perform His healing promises to you. By His stripes you are healed and made whole (Isa. 53:4-5). He takes away this sickness (Deut. 7:15) from you. In Jesus' name, I pray in faith, amen.

Confession of Faith

Father God, I judge You faithful (Heb. 11:11) to keep Your healing promises to me. Your Word says that by Your stripes I am healed (Isa. 53:4-5). You take away this sickness from me (Deut. 7:15). I hold fast the confession of my hope without wavering—You who promised are faithful (Heb. 10:23). I boldly declare that my liver is loosed from this negative report of ascites (Luke 12:13). Fluid may not collect in spaces within my abdomen and cause infections or move into my chest and surround my lungs and cause breathing challenges. Ascites may not enter my kidneys or other organs. This infirmity must leave my body now, in Jesus' name! And because I have faith in His name, I am healed! Amen.

Cirrhosis

Prayer of Faith

I exercise the call to pray to Abba Father for one another (James 5:16) in faith, believing without wavering (James 1:6) for you. I renounce this spirit of death, cirrhosis, the scarring of your liver. I release the healing power of the blood of Jesus to flow through your liver to sustain, refresh, strengthen, and transform your liver from being ill to well (Ps. 41:3). With the power of faith-filled words (Rom. 4:17), I declare that the scarring supernaturally melts and is eliminated from your system, and your liver is fully functional by the grace of God. In Jesus' name, I pray, amen.

Confession of Faith

I declare by faith, without wavering (James 1:6), that my liver is loosed from this bondage of cirrhosis, scarring (Luke 12:13). Based on faith in His name, Jesus (Acts 3:16), I declare that all scarring of my liver is gone by the supernatural power of my Lord. This same power sustains, refreshes, strengthens, and transforms this liver of mine (Ps. 41:3) from weak to strong, from sick to healed. In Jesus' name, I declare, amen.

Hepatitis A

Prayer of Faith

In the name of Jesus, I renounce this contagious liver infection, hepatitis A. I renounce the cause of this infection in you, contaminated food and water, or this disease inside another infected person who passed it on to you. I believe in the healing power of the Lord to cleanse and heal your liver and to strengthen it so that it can function and do what it was created to do, amen.

Confession of Faith

I activate the authority that Jesus gave to me (Luke 10:19) and I speak death (Prov. 18:21) to this infection of my liver, hepatitis A. I renounce the source of this infection in me, the contaminated food and water, or this disease inside another infected person who passed it on to me. I release the power of the Lord to cleanse, heal, and to strengthen it, and I command that the inflammation and all other symptoms leave. I declare by faith that my liver functions as it was designed to work. Amen.

Hepatitis C

Prayer of Faith

In the name of Jesus, I exercise my God-given authority (Luke 10:19) and obey the Lord's command to dominate all living things, including this viral infection (Gen. 1:26-28). I declare that no weapon formed against you will prosper (Isa. 54:17). I release the healing power of the blood of Jesus (Isa. 53:4-5) to flow through your liver to cleanse it from all impurities and inflammation from hepatitis C and declare by faith that you are healed and made whole for the glory of the Lord, amen.

Confession of Faith

By the power of my faith in the healing power of His name (Acts 3:16), I stand against the wiles of the devil (Eph. 6:11) in faith without wavering (James 1:6)—no weapon formed against me shall prosper (Isa. 54:17). I am loosed from this infirmity (Luke 12:13), I am delivered from this curse of hepatitis C (Gal. 3:13), and by His wounds (1 Pet. 2:24) He will sustain, refresh, strengthen, and heal my liver from this viral infection, hepatitis C (Ps. 41:3). By words of faith, I declare things that are not as though they already were (Rom. 4:17): my liver is cleansed, strengthened, healed, free from all viral infection and inflammation. In Jesus' name, I believe, amen.

Liver Cancer

See page 99 under "Cancers."

Liver Failure

Prayer of Faith

In the name of Jesus, I renounce this spirit of death attacking you, liver failure. I declare that no weapon formed against you will prosper (Isa. 54:17). By the power of death in my words (Prov. 18:21), I speak death and destruction to the force and cause behind this failure. With this same power of faith-filled words, I speak life, health, healing, and strength into your liver. I declare that you will not die but live and declare the works of the Lord (Ps. 118:17). Amen.

Confession of Faith

Lord God, it's not by my might, nor by my power, but by Your Spirit (Zech. 4:6) that I am delivered from this spirit of death and liver failure. I declare that I will not die but live and glorify the works of my Lord (Ps. 118:17). I am loosed from liver failure (Luke 12:13)! This weapon of premature death will not prosper against me (Isa. 54:17). With the power of life in my words (Prov. 18:21), I declare that my liver can perform its many important functions, including making blood proteins that aid in clotting, transporting oxygen, supporting my immune system, manufacturing bile to help digest my food, helping my body store sugar (glucose) in the form of glycogen, ridding my body of harmful substances in my bloodstream, and breaking down saturated fat and producing cholesterol. My liver is healed by Your stripes (Isa. 3:4-5)! Amen.

Part 13

LUNG DISEASE/ RESPIRATORY ILLNESS

Acute Respiratory Distress Syndrome (ARDS)

Prayer of Faith

I pray in faith to Abba Father, believing in your healing promise for total deliverance from this spirit of death, ARDS, attacking the alveoli in your lungs. I curse this excessive fluid collecting within them. I believe you are loosed from this respiratory distress (Luke 13:12), and in Jesus' name, I declare Holy Spirit's power and His breath into your lungs (Job 33:4). Amen!

Confession of Faith

In the name of Jesus, I renounce this spirit of death, ARDS, attacking my respiratory system. I receive the creative power of Holy Spirit and His breath into my lungs (Job 33:4). By the healing power of the blood of Jesus the alveoli in my lungs are healed and strengthened. The collection of fluid in them is supernaturally evaporated, and they can breathe in and out with ease, receiving the proper amount of oxygen to sustain my life. I am loosed from this spirit of infirmity, premature death, and from this ventilator. In the most holy of all names, Jesus, I confess it's Your breath in my lungs that sustains me, amen.

Asthma

Prayer of Faith

In the name of Christ, the High Priest of good things (Heb. 9:11), I lift you up to Him in faith, believing without wavering (James 1:6) that you are delivered from this attack of premature death, asthma, allergies, sinus infections, bronchitis, or any other thing that is restricting your ability to breathe. I judge Him faithful (Heb. 11:11) to eagerly perform His Word (Jer. 1:12) to heal you from this infirmity, asthma (Isa. 53:5). Breathe into your lungs His breath (Job 27:3), and let the Holy Spirit breathe with the power of His breath into your lungs (Job 33:4). I believe that you receive this healing power of His. Amen.

Confession of Faith

In the mighty name of Jesus, I stand in faith, believing without wavering (James 1:6) that I am delivered from this spirit of premature death, asthma, allergic reactions to pollen, smoke, mold, animal fur, and any other allergens. I have been gifted by Jesus with all His authority against all the wicked works of the devil, including asthma (Luke 10:19). I am loosed from the bondage of this label (Luke 13:12), and by faith I am free from inhalers, nebulizers, and breathing medications. My lungs can breathe with ease, without wheezing, tightness of the chest, and dry coughing. I am no longer susceptible to sinus and lung infections. I am free from the fear of asthma attacks for You, Holy Spirit, are the breath that I breathe (Job 33:4). Because of Your breathe in my nostrils (Job 27:3), I can run and not grow weary, I can walk and not faint (Isa. 40:31), and with every breath that is within me, I can sing praises to Your name (Ps. 146:2). Amen!

Bronchitis

Prayer of Faith

In the name of the Lord who heals you, Jehovah Rapha (Exod. 15:26), I call forth His healing power into the bronchi of your lungs to deliver them from this infectious disease, bronchitis. I command with all the authority of Christ gifted to me (Luke 10:19) that this python spirit of premature death releases its strangling hold on you. I speak things that are not as though they already were, and by words filled with faith (Rom. 4:17) I prophesy that your bronchi are healed from this infirmity and chronic, wet, and productive cough. I declare that you are already healed (Isa. 53:5); there is no shortness of breath within you, for the power of Holy Spirit is the breath that you breathe (Job 33:4), and you live and move and have your being (Acts 17:28) not by your power or by your might, but by His Spirit (Zech. 4:6). Amen!

Confession of Faith

By Your healing power, Jehovah Rapha (Exod. 15:26), I declare what You have already given to me—healing by those precious stripes You bore upon Your back (Isa. 53:4-5) for my deliverance from this python spirit of premature death that tries to squeeze the life out of my bronchi. But the devil is a defeated foe (Rom. 16:20), and I am more than a conqueror (Rom. 8:37). Jesus, You give me life and life in abundance (John 10:10), and bronchitis is not a blessing but a curse (Deut. 28), and You redeemed me from this curse when You died on the Cross for me (Gal. 3:13). You blessed me with the benefit of healing (Ps. 103:2-3). I am loosed from this python spirit of premature death, bronchitis, free from respiratory infections, and from chronic, wet, and productive coughs. Holy Spirit, You are the breath that I breathe (Job 33:4), and in You I live and move and have my being (Acts 17:28). It's not by my power or by my might but by Your Spirit (Zech. 4:6), and I can run and not grow weary, I can walk and not faint (Isa. 40:31), and I can sing praises to Your name (Ps. 146:2). In Jesus' all-powerful name, I believe that I am healed, amen.

COPD (Chronic Obstructive Pulmonary Disease)

Prayer of Faith

In the name of the Lord, I pray in faith for you. I believe that you are delivered from this python spirit of premature death, COPD, inflammation, breathing trouble, cough, mucus production, wheezing, and the harmful effects of long-term exposure to irritating gases, particulate matter, and cigarette smoke. I believe your lungs are re-created, strengthened, and healed from COPD, and that you will not die but live (Ps. 118:17). You live and move and have your being (Acts 17:28) because the Holy Spirit is the very breath that you breathe (Job 33:4). In Jesus' name, amen.

Confession of Faith

I call upon the power of the Resurrection and the Life (John 11:25), and I receive that same supernatural power that raised Jesus from the dead into my lungs (Eph. 1:19-20). I declare that these lungs that You created in me are free from this python spirit of premature death that is trying to strangle the life out of them. But I will not fear, I will not be discouraged, but I will be strong and courageous (Josh. 1:9), for greater are You in me than the devil is in this world (1 John 4:4). By my faith in Your healing promise, I am healed by Your stripes (Isa. 53:5). My lungs are cleansed and healed from COPD, inflammation, breathing trouble, cough, mucus production, wheezing, long-term exposure to irritating gases, particulate matter, and cigarette smoke. I renounce every negative report against my life and wellbeing, and my hope for the future will not be cut off (Prov. 23:18). For I am strong in the power of Your might. Because I put on the full armor of God, I can stand against the wiles of the devil (Eph. 6:10-11). By the power of the spoken word (Gen. 1), the natural elasticity of my bronchial tubes and air sacs that force air out of my body is restored. Holy Spirit, You are the breath that I breathe (Job 33:4), and in You I live and move and have my being (Acts 17:28). It's not by my power or by my might but by Your Spirit (Zech. 4:6), and I can run and not grow weary, I can walk and not faint (Isa. 40:31), and I can sing praises to Your name (Ps. 146:2). In Jesus' mighty name, I pray in faith and believe that I am healed, amen.

COVID-19

Prayer of Faith

In the name of Jesus your Healer, I renounce this spirit of death and this virus, COVID-19, which has attached itself to your body. I plead the healing virtue of God's Holy Word over your every cell, tissue, organ, and system, and I declare words of faith that they are cleansed and healed from this respiratory illness. I renounce all negative and lingering effects that want to hold on and not let go. I declare that no weapon, including COVID-19, formed against you will prosper in Jesus' name (Isa. 54:17). I apply the power of the blood of Christ over all your vital organs, especially your heart and lungs, and speak strength to your being. I build a wall of supernatural protection between you and death and decree that this premature death shall not pass into your being. In Jesus' name, I stand and fight the good fight of faith (1 Tim. 6:2) on your behalf, amen.

Confession of Faith

I declare the Word of the Lord over myself: *"I will not die, but live, and declare the works of the Lord"* (Ps. 118:17 NKJV). This weapon of spiritual warfare against me and my family will not prosper in Jesus' name (Isa. 54:17). I believe in and receive the healing power of Jehovah Rapha into my every cell, tissue, organ, and system, and I declare by faith that I am healed by the stripes Jesus bore on His back to purchase my healing (Isa. 53:4-5). I speak words of faith over myself that my respiratory system is healed and strengthened, this fever is gone, and it will not return. My sense of taste and smell have returned to me and function normally again. My energy level is restored; this virus is destroyed in my body, for I am a temple of the

Holy Spirit, and I will not share this temple with anyone or anything else (1 Cor. 6:19), amen and amen.

Cystic Fibrosis

Prayer of Faith

I believe that greater is Jesus in us than the devil is in this world (1 John 4:4) and that Jesus gave to us all His authority over satan and all his wicked works (Luke 10:19), including cystic fibrosis. With this authority, I command this spirit of death, generational curse, and familiar spirit of cystic fibrosis out of your body! I call things that are not as though they already were in existence (Rom. 4:17), and your respiratory, digestive, and reproductive systems are healed, strengthened, and made whole. Your CFTR gene is no longer defective but perfected; and the protein that regulates the movement of salt in and out of the cells functions normally; and the mucus, sweat, and digestive juices are thin and slippery as they should be. Your tubes, ducts, and passageways, especially in your lungs and pancreas, are not clogged but open as they should be, in Jesus' name, amen.

Confession of Faith

Lord Jesus, I thank You that You paid the ultimate price for my healing and deliverance from this violent spirit of death, cystic fibrosis. I renounce this thief, the devil who comes to steal, to kill, and to destroy me (John 10:10). I give glory that this is not the end of my story, for You, precious Lord, have given to me all authority over this thief, the devil, and all his wicked works, including cystic fibrosis (Luke 10:19). I thank You for creating me in Your mirror image (Gen. 1:26-28). As Jesus is, so am I in this world (1 John 4:17)—not afraid or discouraged, but strong and courageous (Josh. 1:9). With all boldness, I demand this spirit of death, cystic fibrosis, this generational curse, this familiar spirit to leave my body at once! I do not give you a grace period to remain; you leave me now! With the power of life and death in the tongue (Prov. 18:21), I release the power of creative miracles (Gen. 1) into my respiratory, digestive, and reproductive systems. I receive the creativity of the Lord into them to refashion them so that they function according to God's original design. I declare bold words of faith over my CFTR gene (cystic fibrosis transmembrane conductance regulator) to align itself with the Word of God that declares, *"He sent His word and healed them, and delivered them from their destructions"* (Ps. 107:20 NKJV). This CFTR gene is no longer defective but perfected; and the protein that regulates the movement of salt in and out of the cells functions normally; and the mucus, sweat, and digestive juices are thin and slippery as they should be. My tubes, ducts, and passageways, especially in my lungs and pancreas, are not clogged but open as they should be. In Jesus' name, I believe this to be so in my body, amen.

Emphysema

Prayer of Faith

By faith in the redemptive blood of Jesus, I renounce this spirit of death and emphysema. I release the healing power of the blood of Jesus to flow in and throughout your respiratory system to cleanse, heal, and strengthen them. I speak creative miracles into your alveoli at the end of the smallest air passages, bronchioles—they are re-created and function normally again. In Jesus' name, Holy Spirit is the breath that you breathe (Job 33:4) and you will not die prematurely but live

(Ps. 118:17) to testify of the greatness of our God (Titus 2:13). Amen.

Confession of Faith

In the mighty name of the Lord my God, by faith I declare that my lungs are cleansed from all impurities of death and emphysema. My alveoli at the end of my smallest air passages, bronchioles, are re-created, and they function to perfection. I boldly add to my confession of faith that I overcome by the blood of the Lamb and by the word of my testimony (Rev. 12:11) and that I will not die prematurely but live to declare the works of the Lord (Ps. 118:17). I give thanks to You, Holy Spirit, for You are the very breath that I breathe in Jesus' name, amen.

Lung Cancer

See page 100 under "Cancers."

Pneumonia

Prayer of Faith

I take a bold stand of faith against this spirit of premature death, this infection of the lungs, pneumonia, attacking your health and wellbeing. I renounce the root cause of this infection, unwanted organisms, including bad bacteria, viruses, and fungi. I command these living organisms to die off and to be supernaturally eliminated from your body. I release the healing power of the blood of Jesus to flow through the air sacs in your lungs and to rid them of fluid and pus. I speak healing into your lungs—that they can relax and breathe free and easy by the power of Holy Spirit breathing through you (Job 33:4). Be healed in Jesus' name, amen.

Confession of Faith

By faith in the healing power of the blood that Jesus shed for me (Isa. 53:4-5), I renounce this spirit of death and this infection, pneumonia, in my lungs. I believe and receive His healing virtue to cleanse the air sacs in my lungs from unwanted organisms, including bad bacteria, viruses, and fungi, and to rid them of fluid and pus. I will not be afraid or discouraged but strong and courageous (Josh. 1:9) because the breath of God is in my nostrils (Job 27:3), the Spirit of God has made me, and the breath of the Almighty gives me life (Job 33:4). I believe that my Lord will preserve me and keep me alive (Ps. 41:2), and He will satisfy me with long life and let me see His salvation (Ps. 91:6), amen.

Pulmonary Edema

Prayer of Faith

In the name of Jehovah Rapha, the Lord who heals you (Exod. 15:26), I exercise my authority in Christ (Luke 10:19) and I renounce this spirit of death attacking you with disease and pulmonary edema. I release His healing power to flow in and throughout your entire body, seeking out the root cause, healing it, and making your lungs and the rest of your body whole again. I curse this excessive fluid leaking from your bloodstream into the tissue and airspaces in your lungs. I command this excessive fluid to supernaturally evaporate from your body. Be healed and breathe with the breath of Holy Spirit (Job 33:4). In His precious name, I pray in faith, amen.

Confession of Faith

With the power of the spoken word (Gen. 1), I voice-activate the power of life and death in my tongue (Prov. 18:21) and call those things that are not as though they already are in existence (Rom. 4:17). I renounce this spirit of death attacking my body, and pulmonary edema too. I believe and receive His healing power into my every cell, tissue, organ, and system to search for, find, heal, and cleanse me from all impurities and residues of this premature death. I command with words of faith this excessive fluid leaking from my bloodstream into the tissue and airspaces in my lungs to supernaturally evaporate. I declare by faith that I am healed and can breathe deep and easily because the breath of Holy Spirit breathes for me (Job 33:4). Amen.

Blood Clots

See page 83 under "Brain Disorders."

Tuberculosis

Prayer of Faith

In the name of the Father, Son, and Holy Spirit, I renounce this spirit of death, this infectious disease, tuberculosis, attacking your body. I curse this bacterium, Mycobacterium tuberculosis. I release the healing power of the Lord to flow through your lungs, kidneys, spine, and brain to cleanse them from these bacteria, to supernaturally dissolve the formation of hard nodules, and to command them to stop the damage to your respiratory tissues and cease to form cavities in your lungs. I believe in the creative, miracle-working power of the Lord to re-create your lungs and blood vessels that have been eroded by this disease of the devil. In Jesus' name, be healed and strengthened for the glory of the Lord, amen.

Confession of Faith

By faith in the healing power of my Lord, Jesus Christ, I receive His healing power into my lungs, kidneys, spine, and brain, and they are cleansed from this spirit of premature death, infectious disease, bacteria, nodules in my respiratory tissues, and cavities in my lungs. I believe that my lungs and blood vessels are no longer eroded by this disease but are re-created, strong and healthy, and can breathe freely because the breath of Holy Spirit is within me (Job 33:4), for the glory of my Lord, amen.

Part 14

MALE DISORDERS

Chronic Epididymitis

Prayer of Faith

In Jesus' name, I release the healing power of the Lord to flow into your epididymis at the back of your testicle. I command all the inflammation of this coiled tube to be gone and the root issue be healed, whether it be caused by bacterial infection or sexually transmitted infections. Amen.

Confession of Faith

I declare by faith that no weapon formed against me will prosper (Isa. 54:17). By His wounds (1 Pet. 2:24) my epididymis at the back of my testicle is healed. I have been redeemed from this curse (Gal. 3:13); all inflammation of this coiled tube is healed. By the power of my faith in His name (Acts 3:16), I am healed. Amen.

Impotence/Erectile Dysfunction

Prayer of Faith

In the name of Jesus, I release the healing power of the Lord to deliver you from this infirmity—impotence/erectile dysfunction. I stand in faith with you that you are healed from all physical problems (Isa. 53:4-5), and I release the peace of God (John 14:27) into any psychological issues causing this dysfunction. I believe in the power of the Lord to heal you (Ps. 30:2). Amen.

Confession of Faith

It's not by my might or power but by His Spirit (Zech. 4:6) I am delivered from this curse (Gal. 3:13). I am loosed from this infirmity, erectile dysfunction (Luke 12:13). By the healing power that was shed (Isa. 53:4-5), I am healed and made whole. My body functions according to God's design, and I have no dysfunction. I am healed in Jesus' name, amen.

Male Infertility

Prayer of Faith

In the name of Jesus, I renounce this infertility in you. I release the creative miracle-working power of the Lord to flow through your reproductive organs so that when you are with your wife you are enabled to conceive a child, for the glory of the Lord, amen.

Confession of Faith

I have been redeemed from this curse of infertility (Gal. 3:13) and healed from all diseases (Ps. 103:2-3). By the power of life in my words (Prov. 18:21), I decree and it is established (Job

22:27) that my wife will become pregnant from my seed and bear my child. In Jesus' name, amen.

Prostate Cancer

Prayer of Faith

By faith in our Lord Jesus Christ who heals you, I pray against the enemy's weapons of warfare of premature death, cancer, cancerous cells, and tumors that are attacking your prostate. I prophesy words of healing into the DNA of your prostate cells that they no longer malfunction and overproduce cells that never die, and these cells cannot cling to one another to form tumors. God created within you a healthy prostate and wills to heal you. Your prostate is not only cancer-free but pain-free and functions as it was designed to. I decree a wall of protection from this cancer metastasizing to other parts of your body. I declare by faith you are healed and made whole, amen.

Confession of Faith

I believe in the healing power of the Lord, and without a doubt I know that I know He is both able and willing to cleanse and heal my prostate from all cancerous cells, tumors, and premature death. He heals the DNA of my prostate cells, so they no longer malfunction and overproduce cells that connect and form tumors. No, He re-creates this function within me, and the DNA of my prostate cells follows through with His perfect design of a healthy life cycle. All abnormal cells die off immediately and cannot pass through my bloodstream or lymphatic system into my bladder, my bones, or to other parts of my body. I declare by faith that my cells live and die and submit to God's original design. My prostate is strong and healthy, cancer-free and cancer-proof, pain-free, and functions in a normal fashion free from incontinence and erectile dysfunction, amen and amen.

Prostatitis

Prayer of Faith

In the name of the Lord, I pray in faith for you against the inflammation of your prostate that is causing complication and pain in your body. I curse this inflammation at the root of the problem and command it to leave your prostate. I declare by faith that you can urinate without difficulty. In Jesus' name, amen.

Confession of Faith

I believe and receive all His benefits (Ps. 103:2-3), including healing from the inflammation of my prostate. I have been redeemed from this curse (Gal. 3:13) and loosed from this infirmity (Luke 12:13). By His wounds (1 Pet.2:24), my prostate is healed from inflammation, and I am able to urinate and empty my bladder completely. In Jesus' name, amen.

Testicular Cancer

Prayer of Faith

I pray in the mighty name of Jesus and by the power of His redemptive blood to deliver and heal you from a spirit of death, testicular cancer, cancerous cells, and tumors. I renounce this cancerous label and the destructive power behind it. I release by faith the healing power of the Lord to flow through your testicles, to cleanse them from all impurities of death and disease, to supernaturally dissolve all cancerous cells and tumors and eliminate them from your body, to correct the confusion of the DNA in your testicle cells, and I command that these cancerous cells will not metastasize to other parts of the body. I declare words of faith that line up with God's Word that declares He will take away all sickness from you (Deut. 7:15) and that He will satisfy you with long life (Ps. 91:16) and that the Lord will sustain, refresh, and strengthen you (Ps. 41:3). For your wellbeing and God's great glory, I pray this in faith for you, amen.

Confession of Faith

Death and life are in the power of the tongue (Prov. 18:21) and I will wield this power for my wellbeing. I will not fear or be in bondage to this deadly report (Heb. 2:14-15), for He has loosed me from this infirmity (Luke 13:12). Jesus came to give me life, and life in abundance (John 10:10), and I judge God faithful to keep His promise to me (Heb. 11:11). I receive His healing power into my testicles, the cells of my testicles, and the DNA inside my testicle cells. I declare that there is no malfunction of the production within the DNA of my testicle cells; they fulfill their life cycle and do not form tumors or metastasize to other parts of my body. I decree a wall of protection, the blood of Jesus, over every cell, tissue, organ, and system and declare by faith that I am healed (Isa. 53:4-5) and cleansed from all impurities and residue of premature death and testicular cancer. I declare that I will not die but live and declare the works of my Lord (Ps. 118:17). For He who started a good work in me is faithful (Phil. 1:6), and I allow Him to complete the finished work of the Cross within me (John 19:30). I stand firm upon the Rock of my Salvation (Ps. 62:2), and I claim His life-giving power and strength over myself every day, amen.

Varicocele (Hemorrhoids of the Scrotum)

Prayer of Faith

In the name of Jesus, I renounce this curse, varicocele. I release the healing power of the blood of Jesus to flow through your testicular veins. I command these veins to untwist and to reduce in size and the swelling on the side of the scrotum to be gone. In the name of the Lord, amen.

Confession of Faith

On the foundation of my faith in His name (Acts 3:16), I receive the healing power of the Lord (Isa. 53:4-5) into my body. With the power of faith-filled words (Gen. 1), I decree (Job 22:27) that my testicular veins are healed, no longer twisted or dilated, my sperm count is normal, and I no longer bear the label of infertile. In Your holy name, amen.

Part 15

MENTAL HEALTH DISORDERS

Agoraphobia

Prayer of Faith

In the name of the Lord Jesus Christ, I pray in faith for you against a spirit of fear and this anxiety disorder that has you in bondage to extreme fear and panic. By faith I declare what you already have in Christ—deliverance from this wicked work of the devil (1 John 3:8). I stand in faith without wavering (James 1:6) that you are loosed from the bondage of agoraphobia. I speak and release by faith His peace that surpasses all understanding; you make the right choice today and always keep your mind stayed on Him (Phil. 4:7). By the power of His grace, I pray, amen.

Confession of Faith

By the grace of God, I declare things that are not as though they already exist (Rom. 4:17), and I declare that by His stripes my mind and emotions are delivered from agoraphobia (Isa. 53:4-5). I am no longer controlled by a spirit of fear (2 Tim. 1:7). I am loosed from these invisible chains of extreme fear, panic attacks, and this anxiety disorder. I am delivered from the evil power behind this label, and I now activate the power of a new label over my mental health and wellbeing—redeemed in Jesus' name, amen.

Bipolar Disorder

Prayer of Faith

I lift you up to Father God for inner healing from this mental condition, bipolar disorder. I plead the power of Jesus' blood over your mind and emotions. I renounce these extreme mood swings, the out-of-control emotional highs and lows. I pray that you can make peace with all hurts and disappointments of the past, and the past no longer controls you or dictates the way you feel about yourself or the future. I pray for His ministering angels to surround and protect you from suicide and other forms of self-harm. You will experience the power of the unconditional love that He has for you. In His mercy I pray, amen.

Confession of Faith

Abba Father, I call upon You and receive Your power, Your love, and the strength of a sound mind (2 Tim. 1:7). I choose life this day (Deut. 30:19). I accept Your unconditional love for me (Eph. 1:4-5). I will not be afraid or discouraged, but I will be strong and courageous for You are with me wherever I go (Josh. 1:9). When I am weak and my emotions are out of balance, You remain strong (2 Cor. 12:10). I choose to believe Your promise that I can be free from the pain and the shame of all my past hurts and disappointments (Isa. 61:1). You are my Rock (Ps. 18:2), my strength (Ps. 52:7), and my firm foundation (2 Tim. 2:19). By the power of Your spirit (Zech. 4:6), I can learn to recognize when my feelings are taking over and I need to call out to You for help (Ps. 54:4). Lord, You hear my cries and You heal me (Ps. 30:2). I am not without hope (Ps. 31:24). You have a plan and a purpose for my life (Jer. 29:11), and with You all things are possible (Mark 10:27). Amen.

Depression

Prayer of Faith

In the mighty name of Jesus, I pray that you will lay down every hurt and disappointment and choose to forgive your way out of this depression and any negative diagnosis, choose life, remain in His presence, be filled with the Spirit, find joy and a reason to laugh again, and live your life for His glory, amen and amen.

Confession of Faith

Abba Father, by faith I believe Your healing Word that You love me unconditionally (Eph. 1:4-5). You have good plans and purposes for me (Jer. 29:11). You heal my broken heart and bind up my wounds (Ps. 147:3). You carry my sorrows, my physical and mental pain. By Your stripes that You bore on Your back for me, I am healed and made whole (Isa. 53:4-5). Your joy is my strength (Neh. 8:10), and laughter is good medicine for me (Prov. 17:22). You comfort me (John 14:26), and when I am weak You remain strong (Joel 3:10). Holy Spirit, You empower me (Acts 1:8), and when I pray in tongues I edify myself (1 Cor. 14:4). I overcome this spirit of depression by the blood of the Lamb and by the words of my testimony

(Rev. 12:11). I am not afraid or discouraged, but strong and courageous, for You are with me wherever I go (Josh. 1:9). Amen.

Fear

Prayer of Faith

I call upon the name of the Lord my God on your behalf for your deliverance from this tormenting spirit of extreme fear. I have the faith to believe without wavering (James 1:6) that our Messiah Yeshua shed His blood for you to deliver your mind and emotions from this spirit of fear (Isa. 53:4-5). This spirit of fear does not come from our Lord, and we are not going to shelter it within you any longer. By the Spirit of God, your soul is filled with His power, His love, and with the mind of Christ (2 Tim. 1:7). I hold up the shield of faith and activate the sword of the Spirit (Eph. 6:10-20) on your behalf, amen and amen.

Confession of Faith

By faith in the redemptive blood of Jesus, my Lord and Savior, I am delivered from this spirit of extreme fear. This spirit of fear is not from God, and I will not be in bondage to it any longer, for I am loosed from this infirmity (Luke 12:13). In place of fear, I claim what He has given me—His power, His love, and a sound mind (2 Tim. 1:7). Jesus rescued me from the power of darkness (Col. 3:13). I choose to take up the whole armor of God (Eph. 6:13). I will fear no evil (Ps. 23), and I will not be afraid or discouraged but strong and courageous because God is with me wherever I go (Josh. 1:9). I declare that no weapon formed against me will prosper (Isa. 54:17) and no evil will befall me (Ps. 91:10). When I lie down, I will not be afraid;

when I rest, my sleep will be sweet (Ps. 3:24). For He has put His angels in charge over me (Ps. 91:11-12). Amen.

Multiple Personalities (Dissociative Disorder)

Prayer of Faith

In the name of Jesus, I exercise my God-given authority over satan and all his wicked works against you (Luke 10:19). I renounce this spiritual attack against your mind and emotions. I command these demons to release you in Jesus' name. I renounce thoughts and voices inside your head to harm yourself and others. I command these voices to be silent in Jesus' name. I speak to each of the multiple personalities to walk into the arms of Jesus, your deliver, your Healer. Feel safe and be made whole; be complete and one with Him. I renounce nightmares, extreme fear of the dark, and the demonic activity that overtakes you in the darkness. I declare words of faith that you can connect with reality; your thoughts, memories, surroundings, actions, and identity are healed in Jesus' name, amen.

Confession of Faith

By the power of the blood of Jesus, I am delivered from demons and healed from past abuse, hurts, and trauma. I forgive those who harmed me. I am free from multiple personalities. In Jesus' name, my mind and emotions are made whole, able to be one with Christ. I will not harm myself or others in Jesus' name. With God's help, I deal with reality and do not dissociate from it. I'm loved and accepted by God. I am valuable to Jesus, and I am free in Christ, amen.

Obsessive-Compulsive Disorder (OCD)

Prayer of Faith

In the name of the Lord my God, I renounce this mental health disorder, OCD, and the demonic force behind this label. I renounce spirits of fear, obsession, and compulsion. I command them to come out of you and leave you at once in Jesus' name. I release the power of Holy Spirit to hover over you to comfort and calm you down in Jesus' mighty name, amen.

Confession of Faith

In the mighty name of the Lord my God, I decree words of faith over myself. I am loosed from this torment of OCD (Luke 12:13). By the redemptive power of the work of Calvary, I am delivered from this curse and all the evil power behind it (Gal. 3:13). God has not given me a spirit of fear but of power, of love, and of a sound mind (2 Tim. 1:7). He carried my sorrows (Isa. 53:4), and by His healing stripes I am healed spiritually with my sins forgiven. Mentally and emotionally I am at peace, and all physical sickness is healed too (Isa. 53:5). I have the mind of Christ (1 Cor. 2:16), and with help I can learn to think about things that are lovely and of a good report (Phil. 4:8). I daily cast my cares upon Him and allow Him to take care of them for me (Ps. 55:22). I will not be afraid or discouraged but be strong and courageous, for the Lord my God is with me wherever I go (Josh. 1:9). In Jesus' name, amen.

Panic Disorder

Prayer of Faith

I stand in the gap believing for your deliverance and healing from this panic disorder and feelings of intense anxiety, fear, and terror. I stand on the promise that you are loosed from this infirmity (Luke 12:13) and the sudden fear of death and doom. This spirit of fear (2 Tim. 1:7) no longer has control over your mind and emotions, but you are free, and whom He sets free is free indeed (John 8:36). Amen.

Confession of Faith

Dear Jesus, my Redeemer, I stand in faith believing that by Your stripes that You bore on Your back for me I am delivered, healed, and made whole (Isa. 53:4-5) from these panic attacks and feelings of intense anxiety, fear, and terror. For the weapons of my warfare are not carnal but mighty in God for pulling down strongholds, casting down arguments and every high thing that exalts itself against the knowledge of God, bringing every thought into captivity to the obedience of Christ (2 Cor. 10:4-5). By the power of Your blood, I am delivered from this curse because You became the curse for me (Gal. 3:13). I am loosed from these invisible chains of bondage (Luke 12:13). I am not controlled by a spirit of fear but of power, of love, and of a sound mind (2 Tim. 1:7). I will not be anxious about anything, but in every situation, by prayer and petition, with thanksgiving, present my requests to You. Your peace, which transcends all understanding, will guard my heart and mind in Christ Jesus (Phil. 4:6-7). Amen.

Part 16

Mosquito-Borne Diseases

Dengue and Dengue Hemorrhagic Fever

Prayer of Faith

In Jesus' name, I renounce this dengue virus that has entered your body by an infected mosquito. I declare that the Lord will give you strength (Ps. 29:11). He will sustain and refresh you (Ps. 41:3), and by His stripes you are healed and made whole (Isa. 53:4-5). With the power of life and death in our words (Prov. 18:21), I speak death to these infected mosquitos and a purification of the waters they are born into. I declare that no weapon formed against you shall prosper (Isa. 54:17), in Jesus' name, amen.

Confession of Faith

By the power of faith-filled words, I speak death to this dengue virus living inside of me and in the body of water this mosquito was born into. I curse the negative effects of this against me. I declare words of faith: by His stripes I am healed from dengue fever (Isa. 53:4-5). I take command over my body, and dengue virus dies in my blood and cannot multiply itself in me. You leave my body at once! I curse dengue hemorrhagic fever—you will not survive in me. I will not die but live and glorify the works of the Lord (Ps. 118:17), amen.

Malaria

Prayer of Faith

In the name of Jesus your Healer, I renounce this mosquito-borne disease, malaria. With the power of life and death in my words (Prov. 18:21), I speak death into these malaria parasites that were injected into your bloodstream and into the bodies of water in the community and surrounding area where you were first infected, and I speak life and healing into your body. I declare that no weapon formed against you shall prosper, including malaria (Isa. 54:17), and that the Lord will take all sickness away from you (Deut. 7:15). He will sustain, refresh, and strengthen you (Ps. 41:3); He will preserve you and keep you alive (Ps. 41:2); and by His stripes you are healed (Isa. 53:4-5), amen.

Confession of Faith

By His stripes I am healed from this mosquito-borne disease, malaria (Isa. 53:4-5). I speak death into all the plasmodium parasites that were injected into my bloodstream and into the bodies of water in the community and surrounding areas where I contracted this disease. I declare by faith that not only is my body healed from these malaria parasites, but so too is the water where the mosquito was born. I stand firm on God's promise that this weapon formed against me will not prosper (Isa. 54:17) and that He takes this sickness, malaria, away from me (Deut. 7:15). He will sustain, refresh, and strengthen me (Ps. 41:3); and He will preserve me and keep me alive (Ps. 41:2), in Jesus' name, amen.

West Nile Virus

Prayer of Faith

I call upon the mercy of Adonai; I renounce this mosquito-borne disease, West Nile virus, which has attacked your body. I release the healing power of the Lord to flow in and throughout your every cell, tissue, organ, and system to cleanse and purify them from all impurities of this single-stranded RNA virus. I declare by faith that this weaponized virus from the devil will not prosper in your body (Isa. 54:17) but that by His stripes your body and the waters where this was birthed are healed and made whole (Isa. 53:4-5). In the name of Jesus, I pray, amen.

Confession of Faith

In Jesus' name, I renounce this mosquito-borne disease, West Nile virus. With the power of life and death in my words (Prov. 18:21) I speak death into this single-stranded RNA virus that this mosquito injected into me. I declare the healing promises of the Lord over me and into the bodies of water and surrounding areas where this mosquito was birthed. By faith, this weaponized virus from the devil will not prosper in my body (Isa. 54:17). He takes this virus away from me (Deut. 7:15). He will sustain me, refresh me, and strengthen me (Ps. 41:3), and He will preserve me and keep me alive (Ps. 41:2). In His healing power I believe I am healed, amen.

Yellow Fever

Prayer of Faith

With the authority of Christ gifted to me (Luke 10:19), I command death to this yellow fever virus living in my body and in the waters this mosquito was born in. I declare that no weapon formed against me shall prosper, including yellow fever (Isa. 54:17). By His stripes my every cell, tissue, organ, and system is healed and made whole for the glory of the Lord, amen.

Confession of Faith

In the name of Jesus, I plead His victory over death and disease. I renounce this viral disease, yellow fever, attacking my body. I speak death to this mosquito-borne virus in me and into the waters where this mosquito was born. I declare that no weapon formed against me will prosper (Isa. 54:17) and by His stripes I am healed (Isa. 53:4-5). The Lord will preserve me and keep me alive (Ps. 41:2), in Jesus' name, I pray, amen.

Zika Virus

Prayer of Faith

In the name of Jesus, I renounce this infectious disease, Zika virus. I release the healing power of the Lord to flow throughout your entire body and the bodies of water where this mosquito was birthed, cleansing it from this virus and all its harmful effects.

For those who are pregnant and have been exposed to this virus, I decree a wall of protection between this virus and your baby. I declare bold words of faith that this virus will not pass into your baby, and it will not cause birth defects. In Jesus' name, I pray in faith for you and your baby, amen.

Confession of Faith

I declare words of faith over myself (and, if pregnant, my unborn baby) that no weapon formed against me shall prosper (Isa. 54:17). By faith, this weaponized virus from the devil will not prosper in my body (Isa. 54:17). Jesus takes this virus away from me (Deut. 7:15). He will sustain, refresh, and strengthen me (Ps. 41:3), and He will preserve and keep me alive (Ps. 41:2). In His healing power I believe I am healed, amen.

Part 17

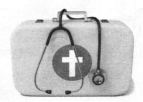

MOUTH CONDITIONS/ DISEASES

Abscessed Tooth

Prayer of Faith

In the name of Jesus, I renounce this abscess in your tooth. I curse this bacterial infection and command the pus to dry up and be gone. I speak healing and strength to the tooth, gums, surrounding teeth, and jawbone, amen.

Confession of Faith

I claim my benefits that Jesus so richly gave to me (Ps. 103:2-3). I accept His healing power into the abscess in my tooth. I receive this healing virtue to cleanse my tooth from this bacterial infection and to give strength and a barrier of protection not only to this tooth, but the surrounding teeth, gums, and jawbone. In His name I pray, amen.

Gingivitis

Prayer of Faith

I renounce this gum disease, gingivitis, plaguing your mouth. I release the healing power of the Lord to flow through your gingiva, cleansing and healing it from bad bacteria, redness, swelling, and pain. In Jesus' name, amen.

Confession of Faith

By the foundation of my faith in the wonderful name of Jesus (Acts 3:16), I believe and receive His healing power to flow through my mouth to cleanse it from this gum disease, gingivitis. I claim His benefit of healing to refresh and to restore my gingiva from irritation, redness, swelling, and pain. In His most holy name I pray, amen.

Oral Cancer

Prayer of Faith

In the name of Jesus Christ I renounce this spirit of death, oral cancer, cancerous cells, tumors, and sores. I release the healing power of the Lord to flow through your mouth and surrounding areas to cleanse them from all residues of death and cancer, to refresh and restore your health and wellbeing. In Jesus' name, amen.

Confession of Faith

I believe and receive the healing power of the blood of Jesus into my mouth and surrounding areas. I am delivered from this spirit of death, oral cancer, cancerous cells, tumors, and sores. My lips and mouth are cancer-fee and cancer-proof. The DNA of my every cell is re-created and is no longer confused. My cells follow God's perfect design of their life cycle, and for the glory of the Lord they live and die as they are supposed to and do not cling together and form tumors. By His wounds, my wounds are healed (Isa. 53:4-5). In Jesus' name, amen.

Periodontitis

Prayer of Faith

With the authority of Christ (Luke 10:19), I renounce this advanced gum disease, periodontitis. I curse this infection of the gums in Jesus' name. I release the healing power of our Lord to refresh and strengthen your teeth, gums, and jawbones (Ps. 41:3). By His wounds your mouth is healed (1 Pet. 2:24), amen.

Confession of Faith

I believe in the healing power of the Lord to heal my gums from this infection, periodontitis (1 Pet. 2:24), and to refresh my teeth and gums and strengthen my jawbones (Ps. 41:3). I believe in the power of re-creation (Gen. 1) and in the power of life in my words (Prov. 18:21), and by those precious stripes that He bore I am healed from periodontitis (Isa. 53:4-5). Amen.

Thrush/Oral Candidiasis

Prayer of Faith

I renounce this candida fungus growing out of control in your mouth in Jesus' name. By His stripes your mouth is delivered and healed from this yeast infection (1 Pet. 2:24). I declare that no weapon formed against you will prosper, including thrush (Isa. 54:17). I believe the promise of His Word that declares, *"He heals the brokenhearted and binds up their wounds"* (Ps. 147:3 NKJV). Amen.

Confession of Faith

Lord Jesus, I judge You faithful (Heb. 11:11) to keep Your promise to heal me. By Your wounds I am healed from thrush (1 Pet. 2:24). No weapon formed against me, including this yeast infection, will prosper (Isa. 54:17). I obey Your command to have dominion over everything that moves on this earth (Gen. 1:26-28). I exercise my God-given authority over the devil and his wicked works, including the overgrowth of this candida fungus in my mouth (Luke 10:19). I am loosed from this infirmity (Luke 12:13). Amen.

TMJ Disorder (Temporomandibular Joint Syndrome)

Prayer of Faith

I activate my God-given authority (Luke 12:13) on your behalf. I renounce this disorder, TMJ, and the evil power behind it. I command your spine; every vertebra, disc, muscle, ligament, tendon, and nerve in your neck and back; your jaw joints; and the muscles that control your jaw movements to be realigned, strengthened, and healed in Jesus' mighty name. All pain and suffering cease for the glory of the Lord, amen.

Confession of Faith

I believe and receive the miracle-working power of the Lord, and I rejoice that His healing power is working in me. By the power of faith-filled words (Gen. 1), I decree and know that my words of faith are established in me (Job. 22:27). I speak things that are not as though they already were (Rom. 4:17), and by faith every vertebra, disc, muscle, ligament, tendon, nerve, and nerve ending in my spine, and my jaw joints and the muscles that control my jaw's movements, are realigned, healed, and strengthened. By His stripes I am healed, pain-free, and made whole (Isa. 53:4-5). Amen.

Part 18

Nerve Damage

Carpal Tunnel Syndrome

Prayer of Faith

In the name of the Lord your Healer (Exod. 15:26), I renounce this diagnosis of carpal tunnel syndrome. I release the healing power of the Lord to flow through your median nerve and to release the pressure from it. I declare words of life (Prov. 18:21): your carpal tunnel is free from numbness and tingling, and strength has returned to your hand and arm. In Jesus' name, amen.

Confession of Faith

In the name of Jesus, I disclaim ownership of this diagnosis of carpal tunnel syndrome. By my faith in the healing power of the name of Jesus (Acts 3:16), I claim His benefit of healing (Ps. 103:2-3) to release the pressure on my median nerve, and by the authority of Christ gifted to me (Luke 10:19) I command it to decompress. My carpal tunnel is free from pain, and numbness in your lower back, hips, buttocks, and legs. Amen.

Confession of Faith

Jesus bought and paid for my healing from sciatica when He bore it on His own body for me (Isa. 53:4-5). Only good and perfect gifts come from God (James 1:17), and so I reject this pain and suffering. It does not belong to me. Jesus has loosed me from this infirmity (Luke 12:13). By His wounds (1 Pet. 2:24) my spine is realigned, any herniated disk is healed, bone spurs are supernaturally gone, any other source of this pressure on my sciatic nerve is healed. Glory to God, by faith I am free from inflammation, pain, and numbness in my lower back, hips, buttocks, and legs. In His healing name, I believe. Amen.

Part 19

NEURODEGENERATIVE DISEASES

ALS

Prayer of Faith

In Jesus' name, by the power of faith, I renounce the spirit of death, the spirit of fear, the power of this negative medical report, negative word curses that have been spoken over you, and this generational curse called ALS attacking your body.

I release the Spirit of the living God to flow throughout your entire being. I declare life and His peace into the nerve cells in your brain and into the very core of your spinal cord. I release the healing power of the Holy Spirit to flow from the very center of your spinal cord and work its way throughout the rest of the body. I command your motor neurons to be regenerated. I call resurrection life into dead motor neurons—they are disease-free, healthy, strong, and function perfectly normally. I come against all forms of paralysis. I command the

Confession of Faith

I confess with my words that I am delivered from Alzheimer's, a shrinking brain, and forgetfulness. My brain is re-created in Jesus' name. I know who I am, who my family and friends are. I remember where I am, where I am going, what I am doing, and with whom I am doing it. I am healed in Jesus' name, amen.

Dementia

Prayer of Faith

In the name of Jesus, I stand in faith believing in the power of our God to deliver you from spirits of death, fear and confusion, dementia, and memory loss. I believe without a doubt that God is willing to heal you of this, and no matter what the world says, God is able to heal you from dementia.

I prophesy words of healing into your physical brain that it is re-created and your memory is refreshed. You can remember what happened from long ago in the past, and you can remember what happened a second ago. You know who you are, who your family and friends are, and you remember their names. You can communicate with ease. You remember what you want to say, and you can recall the words you want to use as you speak. You do not struggle with visual and spatial abilities; you know where you are and where you are going, and you remember how to get there and back again. You are not confused, and you are not lost. All your faculties are intact; you can reason and solve problems. You can plan and organize your daily activities. In the name of Jesus, you hold on to your coordination and motor functions, amen.

Confession of Faith

I believe I am a child of God and that He loves me and cares for me. I trust Jesus for the re-creation of my brain. I am free from fear and confusion. I know who I am, and I know who my family and friends are. I remember names and important dates. I can talk to them and remember what I want to say. By faith, I do not struggle with forgetfulness. I am not controlled by confusion and fear, but I am at peace and happy. I know where I am going and what I am doing. This brain that I have been given serves me well all the days of my life, in Jesus' name, amen.

Huntington's Disease

Prayer of Faith

I raise up my shield of faith and use my sword of the Spirit and fight the good fight of faith with you against this foul spirit of death, this generational curse of Huntington's disease, and the breakdown of the brain's nerve cells. I demand that they leave your body at once in Jesus' mighty name. I stand firm on God's promises of healing for you. I plead the power of the blood of Christ to flow through your brain's nerve cells to re-create, strengthen, and make them whole again for the glory of God. I declare by faith that your physical movements are strong, they cannot find any weakness in them, your mind and emotions are healed, you remain calm and steady for Jesus, and your cognitive abilities remain intact, amen.

Confession of Faith

I declare that I am a strong warrior for the Lord. I am delivered from a spirit of death, and this generational curse of Huntington's disease plagues me no more. My brain's nerve cells are continually built up, not broken down. My physical movements are strong; there is no weakness in them, because my strength is renewed like the eagle's. I can run and not grow weary, and I can walk and not faint (Isa. 40:31). My mind and emotions are healed, and I remain calm and steady for the glory of the Lord. My cognitive abilities remain intact. I lose no ground in my ability to think and to reason. This I believe in Jesus' name, amen.

Parkinson's Disease

Prayer of Faith

I raise up the standard of the blood of Jesus on your behalf. I release its power over this spirit of premature death, this degenerative disorder attacking your central nervous system and the strength and ability of your motor system. I curse this label of Parkinson's and the torment it is causing you. In agreement with God's Word, I declare that you are healed and made whole by the flogging that Jesus bore to purchase your healing. I believe in the redemptive power of the Cross and that you have been redeemed from this curse. By the power of faith in the goodness of our Lord, you are delivered from Parkinson's, your central nervous system is regenerated, your motor system regains its ability and strength. No more do you suffer from tremors, rigidity, slow movements, or have trouble with walking. You are alive and well, in Jesus' name, amen.

Confession of Faith

I believe in the redemptive power of the blood of Jesus, and I align myself with the promises of healing found in God's Word. I declare a statement of faith: I am delivered from premature death, Parkinson's, this degenerative disorder attacking my central nervous system, and the enemy's theft of the ability and strength of my motor system. I bind myself to the work of the Cross and loose myself from the curse of the enemy. By faith I declare I am free from this disease, and I do not suffer from tremors, rigidity, slow movements, or have trouble with walking. I say, "No!" to the devil and "Yes!" to the healing power of Jesus. Amen and amen.

Part 20

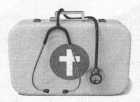

NEUROLOGICAL DISORDERS

Guillain-Barre Syndrome (GBS)

Prayer of Faith

In the name of Jesus, I renounce this spirit of death, this neurological disorder and autoimmune disease, Guillain-Barre syndrome, a spirit of infirmity, and a spirit of paralysis attacking your body. By the authority gifted to me by Jesus (Luke 10:19), I command divine order back into your immune system, and I demand by faith that this attack against your peripheral nervous system stops in the name of the Lord. I renounce all weakness, paralysis, and breathing difficulties. In Jesus' name, you are healed, healthy, and made whole, amen and amen.

Confession of Faith

In the name of the Lord my God, Jehovah Rapha who heals me (Exod. 15:26), I renounce this spirit of death, this neurological disorder and autoimmune disease, Guillain-Barre syndrome, a spirit of infirmity, and a spirit of paralysis. With

His authority gifted to me (Luke 10:19), I command divine order back into my immune system, and I demand by faith that this attack against my peripheral nervous system stops in Jesus' name. With the power of life and death in the tongue (Prov. 18:21), where there is weakness I declare strength. Areas where paralysis has settled in, I declare physical freedom, and my muscular system has been loosed by the healing virtue of the Messiah (Luke 12:13). This Python spirit strangling my ability to breathe—leave my respiratory system at once! Holy Spirit is the breath that I breathe (Job 33:4), and I can breathe with ease in Jesus' name. With the creative power of faith-filled words (Gen. 1), I call things that are not as though they already exist (Rom. 4:17), and my immune system does not harm but heals my body. My peripheral nerves, axons, and myelin sheath are re-created, healed, and for the glory of God they are fully functional for my wellbeing. In the name of my Lord Jesus Christ, amen.

Migraine

Prayer of Faith

In the name of Jesus your Healer, I renounce this curse of migraine headaches that is plaguing you. I declare what you already have—redemption from the curse when Jesus hung on the Cross for you (Gal. 3:13). Along with this migraine curse, I renounce the source of it, even the label behind this tormenting power. I command your spine to be realigned in Jesus' name. I plead the power of the rich blood of Jesus over your brain and brain stem. I command all pain and swelling to be gone. I declare that you are loosed from this nauseating pain and suffering (Luke 12:13). By His stripes you are healed (Isa. 53:4-5) for God's glory and for your wellbeing, amen.

Confession of Faith

By the stripes that Jesus bore on His back for me, I am healed from this tormenting pain (Isa. 53:4-5). I am loosed from migraine headaches (Luke 12:13) because Jesus delivered me from the curse by becoming the curse for me (Gal. 3:13). I claim what God gave to me, freedom in Christ, and whom He sets free is free indeed, and this means me (John 8:36)! I make bold declarations of faith: my spine, neck, brain, and brain stem are in their rightful positions. The source and the triggers of migraines have lost their power over me. All the old negative symptoms have forgotten me and no longer come to call upon me, because this stronghold has released its grip on me. I am delivered from this familiar spirit, and I rejoice because Jehovah Rapha has healed me (Exod. 15:26), amen.

Part 21

NOSE/SINUSES

Acute Sinusitis

Prayer of Faith

In the all-powerful name of Jesus, I curse this illness, acute sinusitis, which is plaguing your sinuses. I release the healing power of Jesus to flow in and throughout your sinuses to cleanse and heal them from this infection and the virus or bad bacteria that has caused this. I command the inflammation of the sinuses to be healed and for the excessive mucus to drain and not to build up again. In Jesus' name, amen.

Confession of Faith

In the name of Jesus, I hold up my shield of faith and rightly use my sword of the Spirit (Eph. 6:16-17) and voice-activate the promises of God (Gen. 1) to heal me from this disease (Ps. 103:2-3). Jesus bought and paid for my healing with His blood (Isa. 53:4-5). I am delivered from this curse of acute sinusitis (Gal. 3:13). With the power of death and life in my words (Prov. 18:21), I renounce this infection caused by a virus or bacteria. I obey God's command to have dominion over every living thing that moves, including viruses and bacteria (Gen. 1:26-28). With the authority Jesus gave to me over the devil and all of his wicked works (Luke 10:19), I command this infection, this virus, and all bad bacteria to leave my body not to return again. I speak to this inflammation in my sinuses to be healed and for this excessive mucus to drain and not to build up again. In His mighty name I prophesy healing into my sinuses, amen.

Chronic Sinusitis

Prayer of Faith

In the name of the Lord our God your Healer (Exod. 15:26), I renounce this chronic sinusitis plaguing your sinuses. I release the healing power of the Lord to cleanse them from infection, to drain them from excessive mucus, and to deliver you from this weakness. In Jesus' name, amen.

Confession of Faith

By His stripes my sinuses are healed (Isa. 53:4-5) and delivered from this curse, chronic sinusitis (Gal. 3:13). Jesus has loosed me from this infirmity (Luke 12:13). I will not forget His benefits, including healing (Ps. 103:2-3). My sinuses are supernaturally cleansed from infections and healed from inflammation, congestion, runny nose, postnasal drainage, pain and tenderness, and reduced sense of smell. In Jesus' name, I am healed! Amen.

Deviated Septum

Prayer of Faith

In the name of Jesus, I release His healing power into your nose to heal this deviated septum. I command the cartilage and bone that separates the nasal cavity to move and to be centered. All breathing problems, congestion, and headaches be gone in Jesus' name, amen.

Confession of Faith

In the name of the Lord my Healer (Exod. 15:26), I believe and receive His healing power into my nose. With the authority of Christ gifted to me (Luke 10:10), I command the cartilage and bone that separates the nasal cavity to move and to be centered. I declare by faith in the name of Jesus (Acts 3:16) I am healed of a deviated septum and free from all breathing problems; congestion and headaches are gone. In Jesus' name, amen.

Nasal Polyps

Prayer of Faith

In the name of the Lord, I release His healing power to supernaturally melt away these nasal polyps. This blockage be gone instantly, nasal airways open up, and breathe with ease. In Jesus' name, amen.

Confession of Faith

By the power of death and life in my words (Prov. 18:21), I prophesy into this nasal polyp to die off at the seed and to dry up at the root and to be supernaturally eliminated from my nose. I am delivered from this blockage, my nasal airways are healed and open, and I can breathe again deep and easy. Amen.

be cleansed, healed, and made whole, and all inflammation of this organ be gone. In Jesus' name, amen.

Confession of Faith

In the name of Jesus my Healer, I have the faith without wavering (James 1:6) to believe in the healing power of the Lord to cleanse and redesign the inward workings of my pancreas. With words filled with the authority of Christ (Luke 10:19), I renounce this disorder between the enzymes and the duodenum. You will work according to God's original design, and enzymes, you will not start to work in the pancreas before you reach the duodenum. You have been constructed by God to function in a certain order, now do so in Jesus' name! By my faith in the redemptive work of Christ (Isa. 53:4-5), my pancreas is healed, it functions to God's perfect design, and it is free from all inflammation. In His holy name, I believe and receive my healing, amen.

Type 1 Diabetes

See page 70 under "Autoimmune Disorders."

Type 2 Diabetes

Prayer of Faith

I stand in faith believing for your healing from this attack against your pancreas. I declare words of faith that you do not have type 2 diabetes but are healed from it, and your pancreas can make a sufficient supply of insulin and can use this insulin well. Your glucose reaches the cells, and the blood sugar levels are normal for the glory of God, amen.

Confession of Faith

I believe in the healing power of the Great Physician to cleanse, heal, re-create, and to strengthen the workings of my pancreas and to deliver me from this attack of the enemy. By the power of the blood from the healing stripes that Jesus bore upon His back for me, I am healed from type 2 diabetes. I declare words of faith over my pancreas, and it does make enough insulin and uses this insulin well. The glucose reaches my cells, and my blood sugar levels are normal. My pancreas is strong and healthy and free from this disease, amen.

Part 23

PARASITES

Parasitic Infestations (Lice, Bed Bugs, and Scabies)

Prayer of Faith

In the name of Jesus, I raise up the standard of the Blood and declare by faith that no weapon formed against you shall prosper (Isa. 54:17). This curse is broken by the power of the Atonement (Gal. 3:13). I have the authority of Christ (Luke 10:19) to activate His destruction against the ploys of the enemy (1 John 3:8). His Word teaches that He created us to subdue the earth and to have dominion over every moving thing (Gen. 1:26-28). I voice-activate this authority over all parasites, especially lice, bed bugs, and the eight-legged microscopic mite Sarcoptes scabiei var hominis mite (the human itch mite) that causes scabies. Your household will not play host to these unwanted creatures. I use the power of life and death in the tongue (Prov. 18:21) and command these parasites to die and their offspring to die; never again will your family be plagued with these evil things. In Christ's name, I believe in the power of these faith-filled words, amen.

Confession of Faith

By faith, I declare a supernatural war against these parasitic insects! They will not live or have their being in my body or in my household. I am a temple of Holy Spirit (1 Cor. 6:19), and I make no room for them, nor do I grant them squatter's rights. I demand them to die off and their offspring to die off. My household and my body (above and under the skin) are free from them. I have the authority of Christ against the devil and his wicked works (Luke 10:19), including infestations of parasitic insects. All the pain and suffering and the damage they have caused stop now! I am healed, and my household is delivered from these harmful creatures, in Jesus' name, amen.

Amebiasis

Prayer of Faith

In Jesus' name, I renounce this parasitic infection, amebiasis, attacking your body. I renounce this single-celled protozoan, E. histolytica, and its cysts and the parasite called trophozoite that has entered your system and made you sick. I release the healing power of our Lord Jesus to enter your digestive tract and cleanse you from this infection and these living creatures, amen.

Confession of Faith

In the name of Jesus, I take my authority in Christ (Luke 10:19). I renounce this parasitic infection, amebiasis. With the power of life and death in my words (Prov. 18:21), I speak death into the single-celled protozoan, E. histolytica, and its cysts and the parasite called trophozoite. You will not inhabit my body or lodge and reproduce in my digestive tract and migrate to my large intestine or burrow into my intestinal wall or colon. I act upon the command of my Lord to subdue this earth and to have dominion over everything that moves, including amebiasis. I demand a deadly exit from my body in Jesus' name! And by faith in His healing power, I am healed and made whole (Isa. 53:4-5). Amen.

Part 24

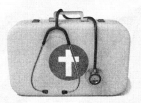

PARATHYROID DISEASE

Hyperparathyroidism

Prayer of Faith

In the name of the Lord God your Healer (Exod. 15:26), I exercise my God-given authority over the devil and his wicked works (Luke 10:19). I renounce this spirit of death attacking your parathyroid glands via this disease, hyperparathyroidism. I release His healing power to re-create your parathyroid glands and to sustain, refresh, restore and heal the balance of parathyroid hormone and calcium in your bloodstream. In Jesus' name, the overproduction of this hormone and calcium stops and returns to normal. I pray in faith for you without wavering (James 1:6), amen.

Confession of Faith

By the power of the blood to heal (Isa. 53:4-5), I stand against the wiles of the devil (Eph. 6:11) in faith without wavering (James 1:6) that I am loosed from this infirmity of hyperparathyroidism (Luke 12:13). I call things that are not as though they already exist (Rom. 4:17), and by faith my parathyroid glands are re-created and the amounts of parathyroid hormone and calcium in my bloodstream are balanced. The overproduction of this hormone and calcium in my bloodstream stops and returns to normal, in Jesus' name, amen.

Hypoparathyroidism

Prayer of Faith

By faith in His name (Acts 3:16), I renounce the underproduction of parathyroid hormone and declare that your parathyroid glands are healed and active as they should be. I declare by faith that you have the proper amounts of magnesium and phosphorus, parathyroid hormone, and calcium in your blood, in Jesus' name, amen.

Confession of Faith

I exercise my faith without wavering (James 1:6) that my parathyroid glands are re-created and are active as God created them to be. By faith in the power of His name (Acts 3:16), I have the proper amounts of parathyroid hormone, calcium, magnesium, and phosphorus in my blood in Jesus' name, amen.

Part 25

SEXUALLY TRANSMITTED DISEASES

Gonorrhea/The Clap

Prayer of Faith

In the name of Jesus, I renounce this sexually transmitted disease, gonorrhea. I speak death into this infectious bacterium (Neisseria gonorrhoeae) that has entered your body. I release the power of the Lord who forgives all your iniquities and heals all your diseases, including gonorrhea and all its symptoms (Ps. 103:2-3). I take authority over the spirit of death that has attacked your reproductive organs. I renounce the label of "infertility" and the emptiness it produces. (If pregnant: I plead the power of the blood over the unborn baby waiting to be born against gonorrhea, blindness, sores on the scalp, and infections.) I speak protection or healing from HIV/AIDS and freedom from a spirit of shame associated with this sexual disease, amen.

Confession of Faith

By my faith in a loving God who forgives my sins and heals my diseases (Ps. 103:2-3), I confess words of faith: my broken heart is mended, and my wounds are healed (Ps. 147:3). I am delivered from this curse of gonorrhea (Gal. 3:13) and loosed from this infirmity (Luke 12:13) of this sexually transmitted disease and it's symptoms. With the power of death and life in my words (Prov. 18:21), I speak death to this infectious bacterium (Neisseria gonorrhoeae) that has entered my body and the power of destruction in my reproductive organs. I renounce this label of "infertility" and the death of my family's future generations. (If pregnant: I plead the power of the blood over the unborn baby waiting to be born against gonorrhea, blindness, sores on the scalp, and infections.) I plead this same healing and power of protection over my immune system from HIV/AIDS. I thank You for taking my shame. In Jesus' name, amen.

Hepatitis B/HBV/Chronic Hepatitis B

Prayer of Faith

I activate the authority of Christ given to me (Luke 10:19) over this hepatitis B virus attacking your liver. I release the healing power of our Lord to flow in and throughout your liver to cleanse, heal, refresh, and strengthen it (Ps. 41:3). I declare that no weapon formed against you and your liver will prosper (Isa. 54:17), and I voice-activate by words of faith that your liver is protected and/or healed from liver failure, cancer, or cirrhosis. I speak to the scarring of your liver to supernaturally melt away and be eliminated from your body as if they never were there to begin with. In Jesus' name, be forgiven of your iniquities and healed from this disease (Ps. 103:2-3). (If pregnant: I plead the power of the blood of Jesus to protect and heal your unborn baby from this HBV as they are birthed into this world.) In Jesus' name, amen.

Confession of Faith

In Jesus' name, with the power of faith-filled words (Gen. 1), I believe in and receive the healing power of the Lord to heal me from hepatitis B and all its negative symptoms. I find the peace of God (John 14:27), knowing that no weapon formed against me shall prosper, including this liver virus (Isa. 54:17). I speak things that are not as though they already were (Rom. 4:17): my liver is cleansed, healed, refreshed, and strengthened from HBV (Ps. 41:3). (If pregnant: My unborn baby is protected and healed from this liver disease.) In Jesus' name, amen.

Herpes (Genital)

Prayer of Faith

In the name of Jesus, I renounce this sexually transmitted infection, genital herpes, rising against your health and well-being. I stand in faith without wavering (James 1:6) that your internal organs, along with your brain and eyes, are cleansed, healed, and made whole from this sexually transmitted infection, and your organs associated with sexual activity and urination are free from inflammation. (If pregnant: I pray the protective and healing power of Jesus to pass through your unborn baby's cells, tissues, organs, and systems during this pregnancy or after birth. I declare words of faith that the baby's internal organs and nervous system are thoroughly cleansed and healed from herpes.) I stand with you that all His benefits belong to you, including forgiveness for ungodly behavior, forgiveness for the one that passed this on to you, and this healing (Ps. 103:2-3). Amen.

Confession of Faith

I stand by the mercy of God, who forgives my sins and heals me from this disease, genital herpes, and all its symptoms (Ps. 103:2-3). I confess with the power of faith-filled words (Gen. 1; Rom. 4:17) that I am healed, cleansed, sustained, refreshed, and strengthened by the redemptive blood of the Lamb of God, Jesus (Ps. 41:3). I choose to walk in freedom from the curse (Gal. 3:13), thanking my God daily that I am loosed from this infirmity (Luke 12:13). By the power of life in my words (Prov. 18:21), my internal organs, my brain, and my eyes are healed and made whole from sexually transmitted infection. My organs associated with sexual activity and urination are free from inflammation. (If pregnant: By His stripes [Isa. 53:4-5] my unborn or newly born baby is free from this disease and their internal organs and nervous system are healed, re-created, and made whole.) In Jesus' name, I stand in faith without wavering (James 1:6) that I am forgiven, and by faith I forgive the one who passed this on to me, and my body is healed, amen.

HIV/AIDS

Prayer of Faith

By faith in the redemptive power of the blood of Jesus, I stand in faith with you that no weapon formed against you will prosper (Isa. 54:17). This spirit of death, HIV/AIDS, is a weapon of warfare from the devil himself against you, but I firmly demand satan to back off—he will not have his way with you. I release the miracle-working power of the Lord to flow through your every cell, tissue, organ, and system to cleanse them from the human immunodeficiency virus, to re-create your immune system so that it can fight off infection and disease, to re-create your CD4T cells to help your body fight disease, and to supernaturally multiply your CD4T cell count to be between 500-1200 cells/ml. I declare words of faith that you will not die prematurely but live and glorify God (Ps. 118:17). By His wounds you are healed (1 Pet. 2:24), your sins are forgiven, and you forgive the one who passed this on to you, in Jesus' name, amen.

(If pregnant: In the name of Jesus, your unborn baby is delivered from the spirit of death, HIV/AIDS; they are full of life, strength, and healing. Your baby is protected from this disease while in your womb, during the birth process, and while breastfeeding. Amen.)

Confession of Faith

I believe in the healing process of the Lord. I first believe and then I see it manifest (Gen. 1), and because I do believe without wavering (Heb. 10:23) I am confident that as I stand before His throne of grace (Heb. 4:16) I am healed in Jesus' name (Ps. 30:2). I make a bold statement of faith that I am delivered from HIV/AIDS. I do not accept this curse, for I have a rich inheritance from God that includes my healing from all disease and forgiveness of my sins (Ps. 103:2-3). I forgive the one who passed this on to me. I call things that are not as though they already were (Rom. 4:17), and by faith in His healing name (Acts 3:16) my immune system is re-created, healed, and made whole. Abba Father has no lack of heavenly supply of CD4T cells, so by faith I believe and receive my

CD4T cell count that is between 500-1200 cells/ml. By His stripes I am healed and made whole! (Isa. 53:4-5)! Amen.

(If pregnant: And in the name of Jesus, my unborn baby is delivered from the spirit of death, HIV/AIDS; they are full of life, strength, and healing. My baby is protected from this disease while in my womb, during the birth process, and while breastfeeding. My baby will not die prematurely but live and glorify God [Ps. 118:17]. Amen.)

Syphilis

Prayer of Faith

In the name of the Lord God your Healer (Exod. 15:26), I stand against the wiles of the devil attacking you (Eph. 6:11). I activate my faith without wavering (James 1:6)—no weapon formed against you will prosper (Isa. 54:17). You are loosed from this infirmity, syphilis (Luke 12:13), and by His wounds your wounds are healed (1 Pet. 2:24). I believe in the mercy of God who forgives sins and heals all diseases, including sexually transmitted diseases (Ps. 103:2-3). By faith you forgive the one who passed this disease on to you. With words of faith in the power of His healing name (Acts 3:16), you are healed from syphilis and all its symptoms (Isa. 53:4-5).

(If pregnant: In Jesus' name, I plead the power of the blood of Jesus to flow through every cell, tissue, organ, and system of your baby to supernaturally deliver your baby from premature death and this disease, syphilis. I declare words of faith that your baby will not die but live to glorify God [Ps. 118:17], in Jesus' name, amen.)

Confession of Faith

I believe in the mercy of God who forgives my sin and heals all my disease (Ps. 103:2-3). I forgive the one who passed this disease on to me. I judge my God faithful to keep His promise of healing to me (Heb. 11:11), and I receive the healing power of His blood (Isa. 53:4-5) to flow through my every cell, tissue, organ, and system to cleanse, heal, sustain, refresh, and to strengthen me from this sexually transmitted disease, syphilis. I believe that with God all things are possible (Mark 10:27) and that I have been given all authority over satan and all his wicked works, including syphilis (Luke 10:19). I renounce all bumps, sores, tumors, neurological disorders, cardiovascular problems, and HIV/AIDS. I put my trust for my life and healing completely in His hands. It's not by my might nor by my power, but by His Spirit (Zech. 4:6) that I can move forward and believe in and receive the power of His mercy (Ps. 145:8).

(If pregnant: In Jesus' name, I plead the power of the blood of Jesus to flow through every cell, tissue, organ, and system of my baby to supernaturally deliver my baby from premature death and this disease, syphilis. I declare words of faith that my baby will not die but live to glorify God [Ps. 118:17], in Jesus' name, amen.)

Trichomoniasis

Prayer of Faith

I plead the power of the blood of Jesus over you. With the power of death and life in my words (Prov. 18:21), I speak death to this tiny parasite, trichomonas vaginalis. I command it to die off within your system and declare words of faith (Rom. 4:17) that by His wounds that He suffered for

Eczema

Prayer of Faith

I lift you up to Abba Father. By faith in the power of the blood of Jesus, I renounce this itchy and painful skin condition, eczema. This does not come from Him, and so we reject it. For only good and perfect gifts come from Him (James 1:17). I stand in faith without wavering you are delivered from this plague, and your skin is healed, and burning wounds are sealed. Your barrier function is strong and provides the protection that your body needs. Your skin retains the correct amount of moisture within and protects against harmful bacteria, allergens, and other irritants. By the power of the blood of Jesus, you are protected from damaging environmental factors. By His healing stripes, you are healed from eczema, and your skin and the barrier function of your skin and your immune system are re-created and heals you and do not harms you. In the name of Jesus, I pray in faith, amen.

Confession of Faith

In the name of Almighty God, I renounce this skin condition, eczema. I declare healing words of faith over myself (Rom. 4:17). By faith, my skin is healed, and with a strong barrier function it can provide the protection that my body needs. My skin retains the proper balance of moisture and protects me against harmful bacteria, allergens, and other irritants. By the blood of Jesus, I am protected from detrimental environmental factors. With the creative power of my words (Gen. 1), I construct a supernatural wall of protection, the blood of Jesus, between my skin and an overload of the bacteria Staphylococcus aureus. This impenetrable wall of protection protects my immune system and empowers it to heal my skin instead of causing it harm. In Jesus' name, I confess these words of faith over myself, amen.

Raynaud's Phenomenon

Prayer of Faith

I call upon the power of God on your behalf to deliver you from vasospasms. I speak to your blood vessels to respond correctly to stress and cold temperatures; your blood vessels can do their job and get blood to the skin. I lift the shield of faith (Eph. 6:16) on your behalf and declare things that are not as though they already were (Rom. 4:17). By faith in the power of His name, no longer do your fingers or toes turn numb or change colors. In Jesus' name, you are healed from Raynaud's phenomenon, amen.

Confession of Faith

With words of faith, I declare things that are not as though they already were (Rom. 4:17). In Jesus' name, I am delivered from Raynaud's phenomenon; my blood vessels respond normally to stress and cold temperatures. My fingers and toes no longer have vasospasms or turn numb or change colors. I am loosed from this curse (Luke 12:13). By Your wounds, dear Jesus, I am healed (1 Pet. 2:24). Amen.

Rosacea

Prayer of Faith

In the name of Jesus, I pray against this skin disorder plaguing you, rosacea. I speak words of faith over this condition and release the healing power of the Lord to flow into the root of the problem and to deliver you from the symptoms of rosacea: the flushing, persistent redness, bumps and pimples, visible blood vessels, burning and stinging, eye irritation, and all other symptoms upsetting you. In Jesus' name, I pray, amen.

Confession of Faith

In Jesus' name, I am delivered from this curse, rosacea (Gal. 3:13). I am loosed from this infirmity (Luke 12:13). By His wounds I am healed (1 Pet. 2:24). With the power of life in the tongue (Prov. 18:21), I declare that I am delivered from rosacea and all its symptoms. No longer do I struggle with the flushing of my face, persistent redness, bumps and pimples, visible blood vessels, burning and stinging, eye irritations, and all other symptoms of this curse because I am free in Jesus' precious name, amen.

Vitiligo

Prayer of Faith

I renounce this skin condition, vitiligo, and command your immune system to stop the destruction of your melanocytes. I demand without option your skin to align itself to the wounds that Jesus suffered for your healing (1 Pet. 2:24). With the creative power of faith (Gen. 1), I release healing words into your skin cells and tell them to produce the proper amount of melanin, this all-important chemical that gives your skin its color. With the power of life in our words (Prov. 18:21), I speak creative miracles into the pigmentation of your skin. I command the pigmentation to be the natural color God gave to you, with no macules or patches of white. I believe that with God all things are possible (Mark 10:27). In His powerful name I pray in faith, believing without wavering (James 1:6). Amen.

Confession of Faith

I hold up my shield of faith (Eph. 6:16), and with the creative power of my words I speak life and healing into my immune system and demand this system to stop destroying my melanocytes. I command by faith that my skin cells produce the proper amount of melanin, this important chemical that gives my skin its proper color (Gen. 1; Prov. 18:21; Rom. 4:17). I verbally activate the healing power of the Lord into the pigmentation of my skin and declare by faith that it transforms into the natural color God gave to me, with no macules or patches of white. By His wounds I am healed from vitiligo (1 Pet. 2:24). I do not waver with doubt and unbelief (James 1:6) but believe that my skin tone is healed and made whole, amen.

Part 27

Sleep Disorders

Insomnia

Prayer of Faith

I activate my faith in Jesus' name (Acts 3:16) on your behalf
against insomnia. I stand on the promise found in His Word
that when you lie down your sleep will be sweet (Prov. 3:24).
In the name of the Lord, I pray, amen.

Confession of Faith

I stand in faith, believing without wavering (James 1:6) that
when I lie down my sleep will be sweet (Prov. 3:24). I cast all
anxiety onto You, because I know that You care for me (1 Peter
5:7). I quietly give You praise because You have delivered me
from this curse of insomnia by becoming the curse for me
(Gal. 3:13). I will both lie down in peace and sleep, for You,
Lord, only make me dwell in safety (Ps. 4:8). Amen.

Narcolepsy

Prayer of Faith

I lift you up to Abba Father for deliverance and healing from this chronic neurological disorder, narcolepsy. I pray that you will both lie yourself down in peace and sleep, for the Lord only makes you dwell in safety (Ps. 4:8). I pray for a healing of your brain's ability to regulate sleep-wake cycles normally, get a good night's rest, and wake up refreshed, in Jesus' name, amen.

Confession of Faith

I am redeemed from this curse, narcolepsy (Gal. 3:13). With faith-filled words, I confess that when I lie down to sleep, my sleep is sweet (Prov. 3:24). I call things that are not as though they already were (Rom. 4:17). By faith my brain is re-created and able to regulate sleep-wake cycles in a normal fashion. I can do all things through Christ who strengthens me (Phil. 4:13), and I am able to get a good night's rest and wake up refreshed, in Jesus' name, amen.

Restless Leg Syndrome

Prayer of Faith

In the name of Jesus your Healer, I lift you up for deliverance and healing from this sleep movement disorder, restless leg syndrome. I pray that you cease to experience this uncomfortable sensation and necessity to move your legs as you try to fall asleep. I pray in faith that you are healed from restless leg syndrome and can sleep in peace, amen.

Confession of Faith

In Jesus' name, I put my trust in the virtue of Your name (Acts 3:16). With the power of faith-filled words (Rom. 4:17), I declare by faith that I am delivered and healed from restless leg syndrome, and my body is at peace, and I can lay my head down and fall asleep in peace and wake up refreshed in the morning (Ps. 4:8) because my faith is in Your name (Acts 3:16), amen.

Sleep Apnea

Prayer of Faith

I stand in faith believing for you that when you lie down to sleep your sleep will be sweet (Prov. 3:24). Your sleep will be uninterrupted as you can breathe with ease, for Holy Spirit is the breath that you breathe (Job 33:4). In the name of Jesus, I pray in faith, amen.

Confession of Faith

By the grace of God, my sleep is sweet (Prov. 3:24). No weapon formed against me shall prosper (Isa. 54:17), including sleep apnea. I call things that are not as though they already were (Rom. 4:17), and on the foundation of faith in the power of His name (Acts 3:16) my breathing is slow and steady, with no interruptions of stopping and starting up again. Holy Spirit is the very breath that I breathe (Job 33:4). I declare the Word of the Lord over me: *"I will both lie down in peace, and sleep; for You alone, O Lord, make me dwell in safety"* (Ps. 4:8 NKJV). Amen.

Part 28

SPEECH DISORDERS

Apraxia

Prayer of Faith

In the mighty name of Jesus, I renounce a mute spirit and this speech disorder, apraxia, and the difficulty it is causing for you. I declare by faith that your brain is re-created, and you can do all things through Christ who strengthens you (Phil. 4:13), including learning to speak with clarity. I continue to speak words of faith over your brain: it can coordinate and direct your speech muscles to move your lips, jaw, and tongue in the correct manner so that you can make the accurate sounds, and your words are spoken with normal speed and rhythm in Jesus' name, amen.

Confession of Faith

In Jesus' name, others can understand what I say, because I can talk clearly, amen.

Hyperthyroidism

Prayer of Faith

By the healing power of the blood of Jesus (Isa. 53:4-5), I renounce this diagnosis of hyperthyroidism and the harm it has caused to your thyroid. I release His healing power to flow in and throughout your thyroid gland to cleanse, heal, and strengthen it. I declare by faith in Jesus' name that your thyroid is not overactive but functions normally and produces the correct amount of thyroid hormone that your body needs. Amen.

Confession of Faith

By faith in His healing name (Acts 3:16), I believe and receive the healing of my thyroid gland by the power of His blood to heal (Isa. 53:4-5). I declare words of faith (Rom. 4:17): my thyroid gland is re-created, not overactive, but it functions perfectly normally and produces the correct amount of thyroid hormone to help my body and not to harm it. In Jesus' name, amen.

Hypothyroidism

Prayer of Faith

In the name of the Lord your Healer (Exod. 15:26), I renounce this spirit of death against your thyroid, hypothyroidism. I release His healing power into your thyroid to cleanse it from this disease and its ill effects. I speak to the underproduction of your thyroid hormone to be balanced, and it produces this hormone in the proper amount that your body needs. In Jesus' name, amen.

Confession of Faith

By faith in the name of the Lord Jesus (Acts 3:16) and by the power of the spoken Word (Gen. 1), I speak healing, refreshing, and strengthening (Ps. 41:3) to overpower my thyroid. I declare things that are not as though they already were in existence (Rom. 4:17). Upon the foundation of these scriptures, I declare that my thyroid is delivered from hypothyroidism, healed, and made whole, in Jesus' name, amen.

Thyroid Cancer

Prayer of Faith

In the name of Jesus, I renounce this spirit of death, cancer, cancerous cells, and tumors attacking your thyroid and spreading to other areas. I release His healing power (Isa. 53:4-5) to flow through your every cell, tissue, organ, and system to cleanse, deliver, and heal them. The malfunction of the DNA inside of your thyroid cells is healed, re-created, and functions to the perfection of God's design. These cells do not over-multiply, but they fulfill God's plan of creation for them—they live and die according to the life cycle God created for them. They abide by this design and no other, and they help your thyroid to live and to function and not harm it in anyway. In Jesus' name amen.

Confession of Faith

I stand against the wiles of the devil (Eph. 6:11) by faith without wavering (James 1:6). By the power of death and life in my words (Prov. 18:21), I speak death to cancer, cancerous cells, tumors, and the confusion of the DNA of my thyroid cells. I declare words of faith that I will not die but live and declare the glory of the Lord (Ps. 118:17) with a re-created thyroid.

Restored DNA in my thyroid cells functions to God's perfection, and my every cell, tissue, organ and system is cancer-free and cancer-proof, in Jesus' name, amen.

Thyroid Nodules

Prayer of Faith

In the name of Jesus, I curse these nodules in or on your thyroid at their seed and command them to dry up at the root and to be supernaturally eliminated from your body with no ill effects. Be healed and made whole (Isa. 53:4-5), amen.

Confession of Faith

By the power of life and death in my words (Prov. 18:21), I speak death to these nodules growing in or on my thyroid. I command them to die off at their seed and to dry up at the root and to be eliminated from my body, by the power of my faith in the name of Jesus (Acts 3:16), amen.

Part 30

TICK-BORNE DISEASES

Alpha-Gal

Prayer of Faith

I believe that we have the authority of Christ (Luke 10:19) and the command of the Lord to subdue the earth and have dominion over everything that moves on the earth (Gen. 1:26-28). On your behalf, I voice-activate this authority and command with the power of death and life in my words (Prov. 18:21). In Jesus' name, I speak death to this sugar molecule called alpha-gal from the bite of a lone star tick. I renounce this curse that it puts upon you with food allergies to red meat and other products made from mammals. I release the supernatural healing power of Jesus into your immune system to heal it from this tick-borne disease, alpha-gal. In the name of Jesus, I stand in faith believing for your healing to manifest. Amen.

Confession of Faith

I stand in faith believing without wavering (James 1:6) that no weapon formed against me will prosper, including alpha-gal disease (Isa. 54:17). I have been given the authority of Christ (Luke 10:19) and the command of the Lord to subdue the earth and have dominion over everything that moves on the earth, including this tick-borne disease (Gen. 1:26-28). With the power of death and life in my words (Prov. 18:21), I speak death to this sugar molecule called alpha-gal from the bite of a lone star tick. I renounce this curse that it released into me— these food allergies to red meat and other products made from mammals. I receive the supernatural healing power of Jesus into my immune system to heal it from this tick-borne disease, alpha-gal. In Jesus' name, I am healed. Amen.

Babesiosis

Prayer of Faith

On your behalf, I exercise my God-given authority (Luke 10:19) over these harmful living creatures, these tiny parasites (Gen. 1:26-28), and with the power of the tongue (Prov. 18:21) I speak death to these parasites, babesia, that have infected your red blood cells. I also speak destruction to the partnership between babesiosis and Lyme disease. I release the healing power of our Lord Jesus to flow through your red blood cells to cleanse them from this infection. In Jesus' name, amen.

Confession of Faith

I stand in faith without wavering (James 1:6) that I am loosed from this infirmity (Luke 12:13), babesiosis, and its connection with Lyme disease. With my God-given authority (Luke 10:19) and the command to subdue this earth and have dominion over everything that moves (Gen. 1:26-28), including these harmful, tiny parasites that have been moving through and infecting my red blood cells. With the power of life and death in my tongue (Prov. 18:21), I speak death to these parasites, babesia. I release the healing power of the blood of Jesus into my red blood cells and declare that I am healed (Isa. 53:4-5), cleansed, and made whole for my health and wellbeing, amen.

Lyme Disease

Prayer of Faith

I renounce this spirit of death, Lyme disease, and borrelia bacteria attacking your health and wellbeing. I declare that no weapon formed against you will prosper (Isa. 54:17). With the power of life and death in my words (Prov. 18:21), I speak death to the borrelia bacteria that were released into your body from the parasite deer tick. I declare that the Lord will sustain, refresh, and strengthen you (Ps. 41:3); satisfy you with long life (Ps. 91:16); and heal you from this disease attacking you (Ps. 103. 2-3). In the name of Almighty Jesus, amen.

Confession of Faith

I declare that no weapon formed against me will prosper (Isa. 54:17). I am loosed from this infirmity, Lyme disease (Luke 12:13), and from the wicked works of the devil that this disease has wreaked upon my health (1 John 3:8). With the authority of Christ gifted to me (Luke 10:19) and by the command of the Lord to subdue to the earth and have dominion over everything that moves (Gen. 1:26-28), and with the power of life and death in my words (Prov. 18:21), I speak death into this borrelia bacteria that was released throughout my body from the parasite living inside of the deer tick that bit me. I declare a supernatural revolution to explode within my every cell, tissue, organ, and system and by the same power that raised Christ from the dead (Rom. 8:11) to cleanse, deliver, heal my body (Ps. 107:20), and to sustain, refresh, and strengthen me (Ps. 41:3). I declare that I will not die but live and declare the works of the Lord (Ps. 118:17). In Jesus' name, I am healed (Isa. 53:4-5). Amen.

Tularemia

Prayer of Faith

By the power of the redemptive blood of Jesus, I renounce this spirit of infirmity, tularemia, attacking your body. With the power of words (Prov. 18:21), I speak death into the bacterium F. tularensis that has entered your body. I speak creative words (Gen. 1) and call things that are not as though they already exist (Rom. 4:17). I declare by faith that you are healed; your skin, eyes, throat, lungs, and intestines are re-created and fully functional for the glory of the Lord and for your health and wellbeing. In Jesus' name, I pray in faith, amen.

Confession of Faith

By the power of faith-filled words (Rom. 4:17), I am delivered, healed, and made whole from this spirit of infirmity, tularemia. With the power of life and death in my words (Prov. 18:21), I speak death into the bacterium F. tularensis that entered my body. I speak words full of life and healing into my skin, eyes, throat, lungs, and intestines, and I believe that in the healing power of my Lord they are healed and made whole for the glory of the Lord and for my health and wellbeing, amen.

Part 31

VIRAL INFECTIONS

Epstein Barr Virus/Mononucleosis

Prayer of Faith

In Jesus' name, I pray in faith over you against this virus. I activate the authority of Jesus given to His followers (Luke 10:19) against Epstein-Barr virus/mononucleosis. We are created in the image of the Father, Son, and Holy Spirit and are commanded to subdue this earth and have dominion over everything that moves, including these tiny, microscopic germs that cause this virus (Gen. 1:26-28). By faith in His healing power, I release His healing virtue into your every cell, tissue, organ, and system to cleanse, heal, and strengthen them, amen.

Confession of Faith

Based on my faith in His name (Acts 3:16), I hold up my shield of faith (Eph. 6:16) against this virus, mononucleosis. I trust in Your promises that You heal all my diseases (Ps. 103:2-3) and that I am loosed from this infirmity (Luke 12:13). I declare things that are not as though they already were (Rom. 4:17), and by faith I am free from fatigue, sore throat, fever, headache, and rash. My lymph nodes, tonsils, and spleen are healed and made whole, amen.

Influenza

Prayer of Faith

In Jesus' name, I renounce this attack of influenza against you. I release the healing power of Jesus to flow in and throughout your every cell, tissue, organ, and system to cleanse them from this viral disease. I plead the power of the blood of the Lamb to protect you from other strains of influenza, known or unknown, that would try to overtake you. For God's glory and for your wellbeing, be healed and made whole from this sickness, amen.

Confession of Faith

I exercise the authority of Christ gifted to me (Luke 10:19) over this viral disease. I declare that no weapon formed against me shall prosper, including influenza (Isa. 54:17). I declare words of life (Prov. 18:21) over my every cell, tissue, organ, and system. I decree words of death (Prov. 18:21) into this influenza. I hold up my shield of faith (Eph. 6:16) to ward off all infectious germs that would try to enter my body. I command all negative symptoms to be gone in Jesus' name. My body is a temple of the Holy Spirit (2 Cor. 6:16), and I will not share His habitat with sickness and disease. I believe in the healing promise of the Lord, and by His wounds I am healed (Isa. 53:4-5), in Jesus' name, amen.

Shingles

Prayer of Faith

In the name of the Lord, I hold up my shield of faith on your behalf (Eph. 6:16) against this viral disease, shingles, which is attacking your nervous system. I believe in the Word of the Lord that declares, *"He sent His word and healed them"* (Ps. 107:20 NKJV). I renounce this disease and lingering residue of torment from chickenpox. No weapon, including shingles, will prosper against you (Isa. 54:17). By His healing wounds you are healed and made whole (1 Pet. 2:24). In Jesus' name, I believe without wavering (James 1:6), amen.

Confession of Faith

In the name of the Lord, I declare that I am healed from this virus, shingles. With words of life (Prov. 18:21), I speak healing into my nervous system and command this blistery rash to dry up, and all the pain and suffering that it is causing me ceases in Jesus' name. I am healed and made whole by His wounds that He bore for me at Calvary (1 Pet. 2:24), amen.

Part 32

WATERBORNE DISEASES

Brain-Eating Amoeba/Naegleria Fowleri

Prayer of Faith

In Jesus' name, I renounce this spirit of death and the brain-eating amoeba, Naegleria fowleri, attacking your central nervous system. With the power of death in our words, I speak death to this brain-eating amoeba and command it to be eliminated from your body, leaving no residue or effects of its existence. In Jesus' name, be healed and made whole, amen.

Confession of Faith

In the name of Jesus, I renounce these spirits of death and fear and the brain-eating amoeba, Naegleria fowleri. Jesus redeemed me from this curse by becoming the curse for me when He hung on the Cross (Gal. 3:13). I fully activate the authority of Christ (Luke 10:19) and obey His command to subdue the earth and have dominion over every living thing, including this amoeba (Gen. 1: 26-28). I declare that no weapon formed against me, including this central nervous system infection, will prosper (Isa. 54:17). I will not die but live and declare the works of the Lord (Ps. 118:17). Based on my faith in His name, my central nervous system is strengthened and in perfect health (Acts 3:16), amen.

Cholera

Prayer of Faith

In the name of Jesus, who promises to remove sickness from our midst (Exod. 23:25), I pray in faith for you, giving thanks that you have been redeemed from this curse (Gal. 3:13), this bacterial infection, cholera. With the power of death and life in my words (Prov. 18:21), I speak immediate death into Vibrio cholera bacteria that contaminates the water and the food that we eat and drink and that has now contaminated your system. Jesus gave us all His authority over satan and his wicked works (Luke 10:19), and Elohim gave us the command to subdue the earth and to have dominion over every living thing (Gen. 1:26-28). This includes Vibrio cholera bacteria. These infectious bacteria will not live in our water, our food, or in our bodies. I declare what we have already been given—supernatural health and healing from Jehovah Rapha, our God who heals (Exod. 15:26). Be healed in Jesus' name, amen.

Confession of Faith

I give glory to God that I am redeemed from this curse (Gal. 3:13), this bacterial infection, cholera. With the power of death and life the words that I speak (Prov. 18:21), I demand immediate death into Vibrio cholera bacteria that contaminates the water and the food that we eat and drink and that has contaminated my system. With the authority that Jesus gave to me over devil's evil works (Luke 10:19) and Elohim's command to subdue this earth and have dominion over everything that moves (Gen. 1:26-28), including this Vibrio cholera bacteria that lives and moves. I declare words of faith that these infectious bacteria will not live in the water that I drink or use, in the food that I eat, or in my physical body in Jesus' name, amen.

Dysentery

Prayer of Faith

In the name of the Lord our God, I renounce this gastrointestinal disease and all bacterial and parasitic infections revolting against your body. With the power of life and death in our words (Prov. 18:21), I speak death to these parasites and bad bacteria, and I release the healing power of the Lord to flow through your digestive system to heal you and make you whole again (Isa. 53:4-5), freeing you from this infirmity (Luke 12:13). In Jesus' name, amen.

Confession of Faith

I activate the authority that Jesus gave to me (Luke 10:19), and I speak death (Prov. 18:21) to this gastrointestinal disease and all bacterial and parasitic infections rising within my body. With this same power of the spoken word, I prophetically release health, healing, and strength into my digestive system. I rejoice because the Lord set me free from this infirmity (Luke 12:13). Amen.

E. Coli (Escherichia Coli)

Prayer of Faith

In Jesus' name, I renounce this intestinal infection, E. coli, within your body. By faith, I release the healing power of Jesus to flow through your system to cleanse it from the Shiga toxin. I speak healing and re-creation to the lining of your small intestine; it functions for the health and wellbeing of your body, amen.

Confession of Faith

By the power of life and death in my words (Prov. 18:21), I speak death to this intestinal infection, E. coli, and to the toxins this is producing within the lining of my small intestine. In Jesus' name, I receive this benefit of supernatural healing (Ps. 103:2-3). In Jesus' name, I pray in faith without wavering (James 1:6), amen.

Giardia

Prayer of Faith

I believe that we have the authority of Christ (Luke 10:19) and the command of the Lord to subdue the earth and have dominion over everything that moves on the earth (Gen. 1:26-28). I voice-activate this authority and command with the power of death and life in my words (Prov. 18:21). In Jesus' name, I renounce this intestinal infection, giardia, its parasites, and their cysts that are making you sick. I speak death to them in your body and in your source of water and food, and I speak a supernatural uprising within your body—the healing power of Jesus overpowers this intestinal infection, giardia, its parasites, and their cysts in Jesus' name, amen.

Confession of Faith

I believe in the name of my Redeemer, Jesus Christ. The shedding of His blood has redeemed me from the curse by becoming the curse for me (Gal. 3:13) and has paid the debt for my salvation, including my healing from this intestinal

INDEX

Abscessed Tooth 206

Acne 244

Acoustic Neuroma 115

Acquired Hemophilia 47

Acute Otitis Media 116

Acute Respiratory Distress Syndrome
(ARDS) 174

Acute Sinusitis 224

Addison's Disease 48

ADHD/ADD 78

Adie's Tonic Pupil 123

Agoraphobia 192

Alcohol Poisoning 110

Alopecia/Hair Loss 49

Alpha-Gal 258

ALS 214

Alzheimer's 216

Amblyopia (Lazy Eye) 224

Amebiasis 232

Anemia 72

Apraxia 252

Ascites 169

Asthma 175

Athlete's Foot/Tinea Pedis 152

Atrial Fibrillation (A-fib) 158

Atrial Septal Defect 159

Auditory Processing Disorder 116

Autism 82

Autoimmune Vasculitis 50

Babesiosis 259

Basal Cell Carcinoma 105

Benign Paroxysmal Positional
Vertigo 117

Bipolar 193

Blepharitis 124

Blindness 125

Blood Clots (Harmful) 83

Blood Pressure (High) 160

Blood Pressure (Low) 161

Bone Cancer 2

Brain Cancer 93

Brain Dead 84

Brain Hemorrhage 84

Brain Tumors 85

Brain-Eating Amoeba/Naegleri
Fowleri 265

Breast Cancer 133

Bronchitis 176

Carpal Tunnel Syndrome 210

Cataracts 126

Celiac Disease 51

Cervical Cancer 134

Cholera 266

Cholesteatoma 117

Cholesterol (High) 162

Chronic Allergies 52

Chronic Epididymitis 186

Chronic Sinusitis 225

Cirrhosis 170

Colon Cancer/Colorectal Cancer 95

Combined ADHD 80

COPD (Chronic Obstructive
Pulmonary Disease) 177

Corneal Conditions 127

Coronary Artery/Heart Disease 162

COVID-19 179

Cystic Fibrosis 180
Deafness 118
Dementia 217
Dengue and Dengue Hemorrhagic
Fever 201
Depression 194
Deviated Septum 225
Diabetic Retinopathy 127
Down's Syndrome/Trisomy 21 155
Drowning 111
Dysarthria 253
Dysentery 167
Dyslexia 86
Dysmenorrhea (Menstrual Cramps)
136
E. Coli (Escherichia Coli) 267
Eardrum Rupture 120
Eczema 245
Emphysema 181
Endometrial Cancer 136
Endometriosis 137
Epilepsy and Seizures 87
Epstein Barr Virus/
Mononucleosis 262
Fatal Accidents 111
Fear 195
Fentanyl Overdose Death (and
Other Illegal Drugs) 112
Fetal Alcohol Syndrome 88
Fibroids (All Types) 138
Fragile X Syndrome 156
Fuchs' Dystrophy 128
Giardia 268
Gingivitis 206
Glaucoma 129
Glioblastoma Multiforme 96
Goiter 254
Gonorrhea/The Clap 236
Grave's Disease, Grave's
Ophthalmopathy, Grave's
Dermopathy 52

Guillain-Barre Syndrome 221
Hashimoto's Thyroiditis 54
Heart Failure/Congestive Heart
Failure 164
Hemophilia 73
Hepatitis A 171
Hepatitis B/HBV/Chronic
Hepatitis B 237
Hepatitis C 171
Herpes (Genital) 238
HIV/AIDS 236
Huntington's Disease 218
Hyperactive/Impulsive ADHD 79
Hyperglycemia 227
Hyperparathyroidism 234
Hyperthyroidism 255
Hypoglycemia 228
Hypoparathyroidism 235
Hypothyroidism 255
Impotence/Erectile Dysfunction 187
Inattentive ADHD, also known as
ADD (attention deficit disorder) 78
Incontinence 139
Infertility 140
Inflammatory Bowel Disease (IBD)/
Crohn's Disease and Ulcerative
Colitis 55
Influenza 263
Insomnia 249
Leukemia 98
Liver Cancer 99
Liver Failure 172
Lung Cancer 100
Lyme Disease 260
Lymphoma 101
Macular Degeneration 130
Malaria 202
Male Infertility 187
Melanoma 107
Meniere's Disease/Vertigo 121
Menopause 121

Migraine 222
Miscarriage (Threatened and Repeated) 142
Multiple Personalities (Dissociative Disorder) 196
Multiple Sclerosis 56
Muscular Dystrophy 156
Myasthenia Gravis 58
Myeloma 103
Myocarditis 165
Nail Fungus/Onychomycosis 153
Narcolepsy 250
Nasal Polyps 226
Neuropathy 211
Nystagmus (Dancing Eye) 131
Obsessive-Compulsive Disorder (OCD) 197
Oral Cancer 207
Osteoporosis 143
Ovarian Cancer 144
Pancreatic Cancer 104
Pancreatitis 228
Panic Disorder 198
PANS/PANDAS 59
Parasitic Infestations (Lice, Bed Bugs, and Scabies) 231
Parkinson's Disease 219
Pericarditis 166
Periodontitis 208
Peripheral Nerve Injuries 211
Pernicious Anemia 60
Pinched Nerve 212
Pneumonia 182
Polycystic Ovary Syndrome (PCOS) 145
Primary Ovarian Insufficiency 147
Prostate Cancer 188
Prostatitis 189
Psoriasis/Psoriatic Arthritis 61
PTSD (Post-Traumatic Stress Disorder) 199

Pulmonary Edema 183
Raynaud's Phenomenon 246
Restless Legs Syndrome (RLS) 250
Retinal Detachment 132
Rheumatoid Arthritis 63
Ringworm/Tinea Corporis 153
Rosacea 246
SADS/Sudden Adult Death Syndrome 112
Salmonella 269
Schizophrenia 200
Sciatica 212
Scleroderma 64
Sepsis 74
Shingles 264
Sickle Cell Disease (SCD) and Sickle Cell Retinopathy 75
SIDS/Crib Death 112
Sjogren's Syndrome 65
Skin Cancer 105
Sleep Apnea 251
Small Vessel Disease 166
Squamous Cell Carcinoma 106
Strabismus (Cross-eyed) 130
Strokes 89
Stuttering 253
Sudden Cardiac Arrest 167
Suicide 113
Swimmer's Ear 121
Syphilis 241
Systemic Lupus Erythematous (SLE) 67
Tuberculosis (TB) 184
Terroristic Acts of Violence (During an Attack/For the Victims) 113
Testicular Cancer 189
Thrush/Oral Candidiasis 208
Thyroid Cancer 256
Thyroid Nodules 257
Tinnitus 122
TMJ Disorder (Temporomandibular Joint Syndrome) 209

Toxic Shock Syndrome (TSS) 148
Traumatic Brain Injury 90
Trichomoniasis 242
Tularemia 261
Turner Syndrome 148
Type 1 Autoimmune Hepatitis 69
Type 1 Diabetes 70
Type 2 Diabetes 229
Typhoid Fever 270

Urinary Tract Infection (UTI) 150
Varicocele/Hemorrhoids of the
Scrotum 191
Ventricular Tachycardia 168
Vitiligo 247
Von Willebrand Factor 76
West Nile Virus 203
Yellow Fever 204
Zika Virus 204

ABOUT BECKY DVORAK

Becky is a dynamic preacher of the Gospel, healing evangelist, prophetess to the nations, Destiny Image author, and host of the powerful teaching program, *Empowered for Healing and Miracles,* featured globally on the *It's Supernatural!* Network on ISN. She conducts healing services, seminars, and conferences globally, and she offers online healing courses.

Becky spent 25 years in the trenches of service for Jesus Christ in an orphanage in Guatemala, Central America. God performed many miracles through Becky during that time, including the raising of the dead. Now the Lord is releasing Becky to equip the Body of Christ in the earth realm on a much greater scale. Becky and her husband, David celebrate 43 years of marriage, have 8 children, 3 adult biological and 5 adopted, 1 son-in-law, 5 daughters-in-law and 14 grandchildren, and live in Arizona, USA.

www.authorbeckydvorak.com

YOUR
Prophetic
C O M M U N I T Y

Are you passionate about hearing God's voice, walking with Jesus, and experiencing the power of the Holy Spirit?

Destiny Image is a community of believers with a passion for equipping and encouraging you to live the prophetic, supernatural life you were created for!

We offer a fresh helping of practical articles, dynamic podcasts, and powerful videos from respected, Spirit-empowered, Christian leaders to fuel the holy fire within you.

Sign up now to get awesome content delivered to your inbox
destinyimage.com/sign-up

Destiny Image